WALKING

WALKING IN AUSTRIA

Brian Spencer

MPC

HUNTER
PUBLISHING INC

British Library Cataloguing in
Publication Data:
Spencer, Brian, *1931-*
  Walking in Austria
  1. Walking — Austria — Guide-
  books
  2. Austria — Description and
  travel —1981- — Guide-books
  I. Title
  914.36'0453   DB16

Cover photograph:The Leutasch
Valley (J. A. Robey).

Photographs on pages 20, 27, 36,
39, 43, 77, 85, 86, 88, 149, 167,
and 188 were taken by the author.
The remaining photographs were
supplied by the Austrian National
Tourist Office, London.

Published by:
Moorland Publishing Co Ltd,
Moor Farm Road,
Airfield Estate,
Ashbourne,
Derbyshire DE6 1HD
England

ISBN 0 86190 196 7 (paperback)
ISBN 0 86190 197 5 (hardback)

Published in the USA by:
Hunter Publishing Inc.,
300 Raritan Centre Parkway,
CN94, Edison, NJ 08818

ISBN 1 55650 023 8

Printed in the UK by Butler and
Tanner Ltd, Frome

CONTENTS

	Introduction	7
1	Tannheimertal	15
2	Damüls	34
3	Oetz	52
4	Leutasch	70
5	Mayrhofen	91
6	Neukirchen	111
7	Kitzbühel	133
8	Kals	150
9	Lienz	168
10	Ramsau	186

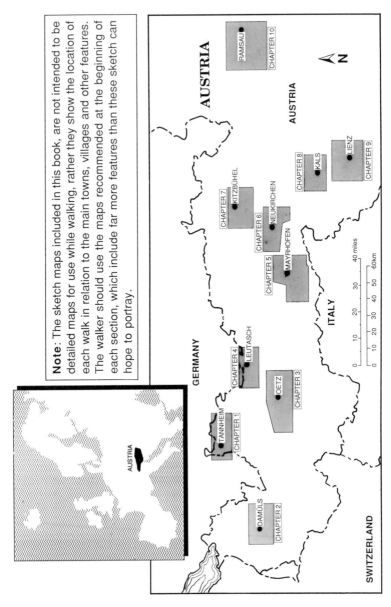

Note: The sketch maps included in this book, are not intended to be detailed maps for use while walking, rather they show the location of each walk in relation to the main towns, villages and other features. The walker should use the maps recommended at the beginning of each section, which include far more features than these sketch can hope to portray.

AUSTRIA

AUSTRALIA

N

GERMANY

SWITZERLAND

ITALY

AUSTRIA

DAMULS
CHAPTER 2

TANNHEIM
CHAPTER 1

LEUTASCH
CHAPTER 4

OETZ
CHAPTER 3

MAYRHOFEN
CHAPTER 5

NEUKIRCHEN
CHAPTER 6

KITZBÜHEL
CHAPTER 7

KALS
CHAPTER 8

LIENZ
CHAPTER 9

RAMSAU
CHAPTER 10

| 0 | 10 | 20 | 30 | 40 miles |
| 0 | 10 | 20 | 30 | 40 | 50 | 60km |

INTRODUCTION

Mountain walking is one of the healthiest sports. Its main advantage over any other sport is that it can be readily adapted to suit the needs of the individual; age or physical fitness need be no drawback.

This guide is planned to suit the average mountain walker, if such a person exists, for walkers come in all shapes, sizes and interests. All the walks should be within most people's ability and most of them are designed so that they can be shortened or lengthened as circumstances dictate.

To some people a visit to the Austrian Alps suggests high-level mountaineering in the realms of snow and ice, but there are literally miles of high-level tracks and pathways available to the non-mountaineer. Most are ideal for the sort of person who wants to ramble amongst marvellous scenery without any involvement in technical difficulty. These walks do just that; all are in close proximity to the high peaks, but none require anything other than a sure foot and a head for heights.

The guide is a selection of easy-to-follow walks from ten centres chosen for their attractiveness and accessibility. Some centres are well known, but others are comparatively off the beaten track. However, all are ideal centres for mountain walking. Others may be better known in winter than summer and so gain fresh interest when viewed from a pedestrian angle.

Eight walks are given for each centre, making an ideal itinerary for 10 to 14 days' holiday when combined with other activities, such as those suggested in the introduction to each section of the guide. Although the walks are designed with families or small groups in mind, some (but only a few) may be a little longer or more difficult than usual. Even so, they should be well within the capabilities of anyone used to hillwalking in moderately difficult terrain. These walks have been added where a more exciting excursion will help the visitor to appreciate the area more fully.

How to Use this Guide

Layout
Each section is devoted to a mountain area or village. The introduc-

tion gives a brief description of the place and also indicates a selection of things to do and points of interest nearby.

The address of the local tourist office is given. These are most helpful places and will be able to tell you everything you want to know about the area: accommodation, bus and train timetables, availability of mountain huts, organised walks and other activities, the state of high-level paths, local weather forecasts and last but not least, details of local concessions and walking badge competitions.

Eight recommended walks in each district are described and range from short walks, often in a valley and ideal for the first day of a holiday, to longer high-level routes suitable for later in the holiday when leg muscles have become accustomed to harder use.

The Walks
A preamble describes the walk in general terms; the route is then described in detail which is intended to be related to the local map — an essential aid to a walking holiday. The map number of the survey, or specially prepared local maps, is given at the beginning of each section. In every case these maps have been used for the preparation of the text and spellings used are those found on the recommended maps. Walking instructions are set out so that each part usually refers to readily identifiable features, for instance footpath crossings, woodland, ridge, hut, etc. There will also be an indication of the conditions around the path at that point: rocky, grassy, muddy, uphill or down, etc. Features such as viewpoints, points of interest, special buildings are in italics. Height differences are quoted when they are considerable, downhill as well as uphill.

Directions which indicate left or right relate to those when you face the object mentioned in the text. The only exception is in the case of rivers, when the direction is always determined as though facing downstream.

Distance and Timing
Distance is given in miles and kilometres. The timing is necessarily approximate, and allows for actual steady walking time, but does not allow for stops.

Height Change
In feet and metres, from the start of the walk to the finish, or to some special feature encountered during the walk, eg from a cable car station to the summit. They cannot give all height differences encountered on the walk, but are an invaluable indication of the amount of

climbing or descending involved. Heights of mountains and passes are quoted to add local interest.

Grading
Walks are graded into three approximate categories:

Easy Walking on wide paths with little change of height — suitable in shoes.

Moderate On well maintained paths. Some height changes, but not exceptional. Boots recommended.

Strenuous Rocky paths. Some easy scrambling. Steep ascents or descents and much height changing. Fairly long distance. Boots essential.

How to Make the Most of Alpine Walking

Mountain Walking
In Austria this does not necessarily mean alpinism. There is a long tradition of footpath building and maintenance, which has given the country an excellent network of high-level pathways throughout the mountain regions.

Paths
Mostly are well signposted and waymarked.

Signposts
Usually give time rather than distance, as this is a far better indication in mountainous regions.

Waymarking
Is usually yellow for low-level paths, and white-red-white at high levels. The colouring may be displayed either as simple painted signs on convenient rocks or trees, or specially made plates or other similar distinctive marks. In some areas, special colour-coding systems are used, sometimes using numbers, to indicate local walks.

Rights of Way
It is possible to walk almost anywhere in the Austrian mountains, either by path or across open country, provided you do not walk through private property or over growing crops, including mowing grass. There is usually no objection to anyone walking across a hayfield once the hay has been gathered in.

Nature

Nature accepts man's intrusion in the mountains better than in some of the lower and more crowded regions. Alpine flowers grow in profusion, so fragile that many are specialised in their own local environment. Animals and birds are there to be seen by the observant; chamois will usually be seen as tiny dots crossing some high snow field well away from danger. Marmots are cheeky creatures, and in some places almost tame. Deer may be accidentally disturbed in forest areas. On high, buzzards and alpine choughs are common while the smaller, seed-eating birds frequent the forest zones. **NB: it is PROHIBITED to pick many of the alpine flowers, and foolish and selfish to pick any.**

Equipment

Should be sufficient for the day. In other words, it should protect without hindering. Boots should protect the ankle and grip the ground without being unduly heavy. Clothing should be light, windproof and above all protect the wearer from cold weather as well as strong sunshine. It is best to wear lightweight clothing with sleeved and collared shirts to keep the sun off unprotected parts of the body. Carry warm sweaters and a waterproof jacket inside a comfortable rucksack.

Food

This should be no problem in the Austrian Alps. Either carry a picnic or aim to stop at one of the many *Gasthöfe* or huts spread conveniently throughout the mountains. Always carry a drink of some kind, and also have some concentrated food tucked away in the rucksack in case of emergency.

Walking in the Alps should be an easygoing affair, especially on some of the higher walks; remember, mountain walking should never be a race. Walk at a steady pace; slow down as you get to higher altitudes, because the thinning atmosphere will take its toll of muscles. The paths are safe provided one acts sensibly; never run, especially downhill, on loose rocks or snow-covered ground.

Accommodation

Accommodation is easy to find, and depends on where you are and how much you want to pay. In the valleys it can range from camp sites to comfortable farms and guesthouses right through to the high-standard hotels which have made Austria famous. Alpine huts are visited on some of the walks; they provide rather basic accommodation, but they are comparatively cheap and the food, though plain, is substantial and always good value.

Travel

The directions for reaching each centre by road usually include a direct route from the Channel ports and alternatives for those wishing to visit Munich or Salzburg, and also for those who prefer a more scenic route.

In Austria, travel on the public transport system can be an enjoyable way of getting to know the local people and their villages. An excellent system of post buses serves most of the mountain valleys, often going to surprisingly high altitudes. They run to fairly strict schedules, but not quite as rigid as the Swiss. Bus drivers are friendly people with a great fund of local knowledge, usually keen to get to know strangers using their route. Long-distance buses follow the major roads and are a useful contact between the main centres of population. Trains run to or close to, several of the centres in the guide. Mayrhofen is especially favoured, being served by the Zillertalbahn steam railway.

Details of timetables are available from the local tourist office. Check if there are any special or extra holiday buses running outside normal schedules.

Cable cars and chairlifts take the drudgery out of most of the steepest ascents mentioned in this guide and are a welcome aid to all except the most ardent purist.

Organised Walks

Many holiday areas have a programme of guided walks to suit all tastes and abilities. These are advertised at tourist information offices. Most resorts issue walking badges which are a popular means of recalling a holiday spent in the mountains. A special card is issued by the sponsoring tourist office, stamps are collected by individual walkers at *Gasthöfe* and mountain huts throughout the district. Once the requisite number of stamps have been collected, the holder is entitled to a badge. This scheme encourages walkers to reach less known parts of the district.

Mountain Safety

Mountain walking is one of the best forms of exercise, and mountains are places for rest and relaxation, but it is absolutely essential to follow certain rules:

1 • Make sure that you and your party are fit to do the walk.

11

2 • Plan your route and check on weather conditions.

3 • Be properly equipped for the walk.

4 • Always tell someone in advance about your planned route, or leave a note where it can be found.

5 • Do not rush. Take your time, especially at high altitudes.

6 • Keep to the marked path.

7 • Do not dislodge stones.

8 • Never be afraid to turn back.

9 • Keep calm if something goes wrong. If there is an accident send for help, making sure to specify exactly where it occurred.

10 • Keep the mountains tidy and do not pick flowers.

NB: Although information on features, condition of paths etc is correct on going to press, changes may take place. Always check locally concerning current conditions.

Useful Information

Tourist Offices

UK
Austrian National Tourist Office
30 St George Street
London W1R 9FA
☎ (01) 629 0461

USA
Austrian National Tourist Office
500 Fifth Avenue
20th Floor, Suite 2009
New York, NY 10110
☎ (212) 944 6880

Austrian National Tourist Office
3440 Wilshire Boulevard, Suite 906
Los Angeles
California 90010
☎ (213) 380 3309

These will provide information on accommodation, maps, rail/bus travel, and are generally helpful on giving advice for holiday planning.

Foreign Language Broadcast

Austrian Radio broadcasts news bulletins in French and English on the first programme everyday from 8.05am to 8.15am. 'Blue Danube Radio' broadcasts daily in English and French from 7.00am to 10.00am and noon to 2.00pm, also at 6.00pm to 7.55pm on 102.2 MHz FM. This programme is restricted to Vienna.

Public and Bank Holidays
New Year's Day (1 January), Epiphany (6 January), Easter Monday, Labour Day (1 May), Ascension Day, Whit Monday, Corpus Christi Day, Assumption of the Virgin (15 August), National Holiday (26 October), All Saints' Day (1 November), Feast of the Immaculate Conception (8 December), Christmas Day and Boxing Day (25 and 26 December).

Hints for Motorists
Most traffic regulations and road signs are similar to those in other European countries.

Speed Limits   Maximum speed between place name signs 50kmh (35mph) if not otherwise stipulated.

Seat Belts   The wearing of seat belts is obligatory, including rear seat belts where fitted.

Drunken Driving   (permissible alcohol limit 0.8 per cent), is punishable by a maximum fine of AS5,000, (in 1987), and confiscation of driving licence.

Children   Children under 12 years of age must sit on the back seat, not next to the driver.

Medical Care
Chemist shops (*Apotheken*) operate on a rota system for night and Sunday duty. Information about emergency medical service (*Ärztenotdienst*) is obtainable from the local police station, as well as from the telephone directory.

Maps
Available through the Swiss National Tourist Office or:

Edward Stanford Ltd
12–14 Long Acre
London WC2

Rand McNally Map Store
10 E 53rd Street
New York

McCarta Ltd
The Map & Guide Shop
122 Kings Cross Road
London WC1X 9DS

The Map Shop
15 High Street
Upton-upon-Severn
Worcs. WR8 0HJ

Insurance

Specialist insurance for mountain holidays can be obtained from your local broker, or in the UK from:

West Mercia Insurance Services
High Street
Wombourne
Wolverhampton WV5 9DN

NB: mountain rescue in Austria can be expensive; it is not always free, as it is in Britain and some other countries.

German Words Used in Place Names

The following list includes many geographical terms which are commonly used in place names in Austria. A knowledge of them will help the visitor when map reading etc. In the text we have tried to avoid mixed German/English names like 'Goldriedsee lake', 'Leitherbach stream' or Ködnitztal valley', instead using the German-only version, which is the one found on maps and signposts.

Note also that some walks refer to terms such as 'point 1371'. These are spot heights in metres, marked on the map for features that have no other means of identification.

-ache	river	*-horn*	pointed peak
-alm	alpine meadow (often a woodland clearing)	*-joch*	pass, col
		-kees	glacier (local dialect word)
-alp	high meadow	*-klamm*	narrow gorge
-bach	brook, stream	*Ober-*	upper
-bachl	small stream	*-sattel*	saddle, col
-blick	view	*-scharte*	very narrow rocky col/pass
-brücke	bridge		
-dorf	village	*-see*	lake
Gasthof		*-speicher*	reservoir
(plural		*-spitze*	peak
Gasthöfe)	small restaurant	*-steig*	path
-gletscher	glacier	*-tal*	valley
-grund	side valley (local dialect, literally means 'ground')	*Unter-*	lower
		-wald	forest
		-wand	wall
-höhe	height, hill	*-weg*	way, path

1 TANNHEIMERTAL

Map

Kompass Wanderkarte (1:50,000 series) Sheet 4; Füssen-Ausser-fern.

How to Get There

Road

1 • **Direct Route** East on the German *Autobahn* number 8 (E11) to Augsburg, then south on road 17 via Landsberg, Peiting and Schwangau to the Austro-German border at Füssen, then the Austrian road 314 to Reutte and the Gaicht Pass.

2 • As above to Füssen, then via Pfronten and enter the Tannheimertal at Grän.

3 • South along the German *Autobahn* E4 to Basel in Switzerland. East via Zurich to the Arlberg Pass; into the Inn valley on the E17, North-east and north to Reutte on road 314 to Reutte or Füssen. Then via the Gaicht Pass as 1.

Rail

Trans-European services via Munich then local train to Reutte followed by the post bus.

Air

International airport at Munich. Rail and post bus service via Reutte or Füssen.

The Area

It is many years since the valley was completely filled by fir trees which prompted the early settlers to dub it the 'Home of the Fir Trees', or Tannheimertal. They hacked the trees out of the flat, easily farmed valley bottom and now only the steeper ground shows what this valley was like before man came along. For once, the hand of man has improved rather than spoilt the scenic beauty of the place. If it were still heavily forested, no doubt Tannheimertal would be a gloomy shut-in place, but with the clearances, the fertile sunny valley is counterpoint to the tree-lined slopes. Above the tree line are the towering dolomitic peaks of giants such as the Rote Fluh, Aggenstein or the Geisshorn.

Despite their seemingly sheer-sided appearance, many of the dramatic peaks and ridges are within the capabilities of strong hill-walkers. Some have broad, easy-to-follow paths across or below their crests and some, like the Rote Fluh, only become difficult in their final stages, where cautious walkers must be content to climb to within the last hundred feet or so of their summits.

Miles of lower level paths wander either along the sides of the Tannheimertal or up attractive side valleys. Anyone whose aspirations are not necessarily aimed towards the high points, can revel in the freedom of this region. Emerald-green mountain lakes are found almost hidden at the top of several side valleys. They make an ideal goal on a hot day when a shady walk followed by a picnic and a bathe are a better proposition than an attempt on one of the summits in the area.

Three chairlifts and a cable car will take most of the effort away from reaching the ridges lining the eastern half of the valley.

A 'Hiking Badge' competition encourages participants to explore all the lesser known parts of the Tannheimertal. The scheme is to collect stamps which might mean the difference between say, a silver or gold 'medal'. An innocent pastime, but one which seems to appeal to even the most cynical.

Tennis, swimming — indoor and out, mini- golf or simply watching the local wood-carvers at work, are all activities designed to fill the intervals between walking in the mountains and on the hillsides of this valley of the pine trees.

Useful Information

Tourist Office
Fremdenverkehrsverband
A–6675 Tannheim
☎ 0 5675/6220 or ☎ 0 5675/6303

Accommodation
Ranges from four-star hotels to farmhouse *Gasthöfe* and rented apartments.Camping at Haldensee, Nesselwängle and Grän.

Chairlifts
Füssenjoch Claims to be the longest single-stage chairlift in Eu-

rope. Lower station at Grän. Useful if climbing the Aggenstein or the Grosse Schlicke.

Neuner Kopf Two-stage lift. Useful for gaining access to the Saalfelder Hohenweg path.

Cable Car
Hahnenkamm Winter skiing area. Lift gains access to a high-level path beneath the Rote Fluh.

Recommended Local Excursions
Hohenschwangau For Neuschwanstein, legendary nineteenth-century castle of 'Mad' Ludwig of Bavaria.

Kleiner Walsertal Duty- free enclave only accessible via Oberstdorf in Germany.

Forggensee Bavarian lake district — north of Füssen. Lake cruises, bathing.

Walking amidst glorious alpine scenery

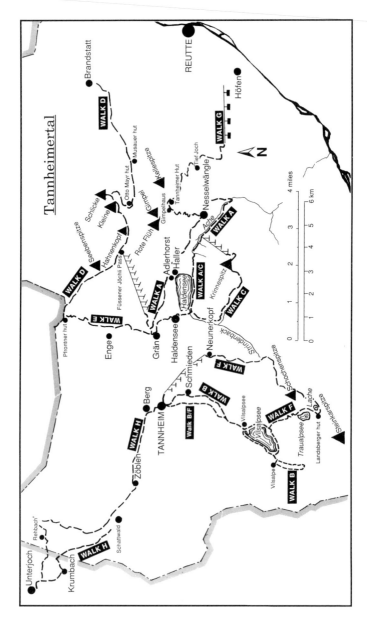

Tannheimertal

Brandstatt
WALK D
Schlicke
Musauer hut
Otto Mayr hut
Kleine
Kellespitze
Seebenspitze
Hähnenkopf
Gimpel
Gimpelhaus
Rote Flüh
Füssener Jöchli Pass
WALK D
Adlerhorst
Haller
WALK A
WALK E
Pfrontner hut
Enge
Grän
Haldensee
Haldensee
WALK A/C
Krinnespitze
WALK C
Neunerkopf
Strindenbach
Berg
WALK H
TANNHEIM
Schmieden
WALK F
WALK B
Walk B/F
Zöblen
Vilsalpsee
Schochenspitze
Vilsalpsee
Traualpsee
Lache
Landsberger hut
WALK F
Steinkarspitze
WALK B
Schattwald
WALK H
Rehbach'
Unterjoch
Krumbach

REUTTE
Höfen
WALK G
Tannheimer Hut
Tief Joch
Nesselwängle
Ache
WALK A

N

0 1 2 3 4 5 6 km
0 1 2 3 4 miles

A • HALDENSEE AND NESSELWÄNGLE

9$^1/_2$ miles (15km). $^3/_4$ hours. Easy.

The purpose of this walk is to act as an introduction to the Tannheim valley. As well as gently preparing the visitor for alpine walking, it also follows paths where the views range up and down the valley, taking in all the nearby peaks and ridges. The vista of the broad lower valley can be seen from the higher sections of the walk, offering tempting possibilities for more mountain walking than can be covered during the normal length of holiday allotted to most of us.

Starting from the village of Haldensee, the route follows an easy, almost level path all the way past Haldensee's lake as far as Nesselwängle. Easy climbing along the wooded slopes above the village leads on to Grän and short walk back to Haldensee village.

The walk can easily be extended along the valley from Grän, returning by way of Tannheim, the central village in the valley.

The Route

1 ☐ From Haldensee follow the lane opposite the village church, past the camp site and on towards the southern shore of the lake.

Despite much modern development, there are several ancient farm buildings in and around Haldensee. The church is spartan in its decor, but arguably the more attractive as a result.

2 ☐ Walk to the right, round the lake as far as the bridge crossing one of the side streams. Take the left of two tracks and walk around the perimeter of meadowland towards a group of farm buildings and the Krinnespitz chairlift.

3 ☐ Pass the lower station and follow the stream past the camp site.

4 ☐ Still following the stream side path, walk up to the main road.

The Rote Fluh — 6,928ft (2,111m) and Kellespitz — 7,352ft (2,240m) dominate the valley's northern skyline. Like the rest of the peaks in the area, they are composed of dolomitic limestones laid down in a tropical sea millions of years ago.

5 ☐ Cross the road and follow the track bearing left above the meadows. Skirt the edge of the pine forest.

6 ☐ Bear left at a path junction and walk through Nesselwängle.

Nesselwängle with its selection of hotels and restaurants could make a suitable lunch stop. The church is worth a visit to see its baroque interior. Outside there is a macabre memorial from World War I.

7 ☐ Follow the track parallel to and above the road, in and out of sparse woodland along the upper edge of meadows and grazings, and skirt above Haller.

The old post-hotel in Haller was once visited by the late President Roosevelt's mother, who caught a monster pike in the nearby lake — its stuffed carcass is there for all to see.

8 ☐ Climb up through the forest to the Adlerhorst restaurant and bear left across the rocky hillside.

9 ☐ Descend as far as Grän and turn left along the road for about ¹/₄ mile (0.4km).

10 ☐ Turn left along the side road back to Haldensee.

11 ☐ Hardier walkers may wish to extend the walk down the valley to Berg, then cross over to Tannheim and return by way of Tannheim and a quiet field track back to Haldensee.

Ski 'walking' in winter can be as much fun as summer walking

B • VILSALPSEE

11¹/₂ miles (18.5km). 5 hours. Easy

The Vilsalpsee is without doubt the jewel in Tannheimertal's crown. The emerald water of the lake, surrounded by pine-clad slopes beneath rocky peaks, is everyone's idea of the perfect alpine scene. Two friendly eating places act as highlights for this walk.

An easy path follows the forested valley until suddenly the glorious vista of lake and mountains open in front of you. A lakeside stroll leads into the narrowing upper valley which ends in a dramatic almost blank wall, down which cascades a lace-like waterfall. The return journey is along the opposite side of the valley back to Tannheim village.

The Route

1 ☐   From the centre of Tannheim village follow the signposted track to Schmieden.

Schmieden, a farm settlement reasonably untouched by modern development, has a Gasthof *with a friendly local atmosphere.*

2 ☐   Follow the track away from the farmhouses and go down to the valley road.

3 ☐   Turn left, walking parallel to the road and follow the track in and out of forest, all the way to Vilsalpsee.

A Gasthof *and restaurant offer refreshment. Both are excellent, although the former has the better atmosphere. Trout fresh from the lake are a speciality.*

4 ☐   Turn left and follow the lakeside track beneath the wooded slopes of Blässe.

A memorial stone at the side of the track tells of a winter avalanche in this idyllic spot — a warning that nature can often be cruel.

5 ☐   Walk as far as the lake head and turn left on the track leading to the Vilsalpe farm.

Vilsalpe is a farm used only in summer when cattle are brought up from the main valley to graze. Refreshments are usually on sale.

6 □   Continue by footpath up the wooded valley until progress is stopped by a sheer rocky wall.

The waterfall at the valley head flows from a tiny lake, the Alpesee, set in a hollow beneath the Steinkarspitze — 6,784ft (2,067m). The summit is hidden behind the walled-in valley head.

7 □   Turn right and cross the rocky valley floor. Follow the path, faint in places, through scrubby forest and tiny flower-bedecked meadows.

8 □   Pass the Vilsalpe farm for a second time and turn left on reaching the lake.

9 □   Follow the rocky shore back to the road end.

10 □   Walk down the road for about $\frac{1}{4}$ mile (1.2km) and turn left on a track which crosses the river and wanders quietly through the forest around the Rossberg hillside.

11 □   Rejoin the road and follow it down to Tannheim village.

There is a good view of the village clustered around its onion-domed church. Opposite is Grän and the Engetal where the side road crosses a low wooded col marking the frontier with Germany.

To the right of the col, the Aggenstein marks the western end of a limestone ridge which includes such local giants as the Rote Fluh, Gimpel and Kellespitze.

C • THE KRINNESPITZ

5$\frac{1}{2}$ miles (8.8km). 4 hours. Moderate.
1,552ft (473m) ascent, 4,238ft (878m) descent.

The Krinnespitz dominates the southern skyline above Haldensee's lake, it is a real mountain, but one which is easily climbed. A chairlift from Nesselwängle takes much of the effort out of climbing the steep lower hillsides and an exciting path leads to the narrow summit ridge.

From the airy grass-covered summit, the view covers the whole of the Tannheim valley and its surrounding peaks.

A word of warning to anyone who does not have a good head for heights. The scramble up the final ridge by way of the Gamsbocksteig footpath is exposed in places and is not recommended in a high wind. The initial descent from the summit is over a steep grassy slope and can be dangerous in wet weather if taken direct.

Below the summit the going is much easier, a mountain hut offers shelter and refreshment before the final downhill walk along an increasingly easy forest track, which joins the main valley above Haldensee.

The Route

1 ☐   Take the Krinnespitz chairlift from Nesselwängle to its upper station.

2 ☐   Climb to the left away from the chairlift through the last scrubby pines of the upper forest. Aim for the craggy hillside in front.

3 ☐   Turn left up the gradually narrowing ridge. Difficult and exposed sections are protected by a wire rope.

4 ☐   Climb the final stages of the Gamsbocksteig path to the grassy summit.

A large cross, in keeping with most alpine summits, decorates the top of the Krinnespitz. The view makes the effort of the climb worthwhile.

5 ☐   Bear left, then right down the steep grassy south- western slope of the mountain. Zigzagging takes the effort and most of the danger out of this potentially slippery slope.

6 ☐   Go to the right across alpine pasture towards the welcome sight of the Nesselwängler Ödenalpe hut.

7 ☐   Turn left downhill by footpath, away from the hut and follow the narrow wooded side valley into the Strindenbach valley.

8 ☐   Join a forest track and follow it round the brow of the steep hillside.

9 ☐   Ignoring paths and tracks on the left, walk down the valley towards the Tannheimertal.

10 ☐   Turn right on a path skirting the southern shore of the lake.

11 ☐   Keep right to follow a field track beyond the lake. Go past the farmsteads at Schmitte to the chairlift.

Nesselwängle village is above the meadows opposite the Krinnespitz chairlift if a visit to the local shops is required.

D • GROSSE SCHLICKE AND THE REINTAL

7 miles (11km). 5 hours. Moderate/Strenuous.
801ft (224m) ascent, 3,807ft (1,160m) descent.

As this walk finishes in the Lech valley below Reutte, careful planning will be necessary to arrange transport back from Rosschläg, either by post bus or car. After gaining the initial height to the Füssener-Jöchli Pass by Europe's longest chairlift, the route passes beneath a series of rocky peaks before climbing the Grosse Schlicke — 6,761ft (2,060m). The Otto Mayr hut will make a convenient lunch stop before the long final descent is made along the Reintal, a mysterious and densely forested valley where man's only impact is in cutting down mature trees or repairing the rough valley track. At the bottom of the valley the change is abrupt as the path enters the broad, flat, fertile Lech with its trim farms and lush meadows.

The Route

1 □   Take the chairlift from above Grän to the Füssener-Jöchli Pass.

Riding on the chairlift can be almost soporific, the only sound being the occasional clatter as the chair's supporting arm negotiates restraining pulleys, or the gentle clanging of cowbells round the necks of animals grazing on the flowery alpine pasture. In the lower stages, the cable climbs at treetop height through dense pine forest.

2 □   Turn right away from the upper station along the prominent hilltop path, later bearing left towards a narrow gap in the far ridge.

3 □   Go through the gap. Descend slightly then take a left turn below the Hahnenkopf.

4 □   Follow the contours across the hillside to a path junction on the Vilser Scharte col at point 1816.

5 □   Walk ahead, uphill over rocky scrub-covered ground traversing below the Kleine Schlicke.

6 □   Climb the steep last hundred feet or so to the summit of Grosse Schlicke — 6,761ft (2,060m).

The best view is to the south and covers the awesome north walls of Gimpel — 7,142ft (2,176m) and Kellespitze — 7,352ft (2,240m), the highest and most dramatic peaks on the north side of the Tannheim valley.

7 ☐   Walk carefully down the south slope of Schlicke. Ignore the first path on the right which was used for the ascent, but turn right at the second.

8 ☐   Follow the contours above the tree line to a path junction and turn left, downhill.

9 ☐   Walk through the trees to the Otto Mayr hut.

The Otto Mayr hut can be used for a late lunch stop or for a drink.

10 ☐   Left from the hut down to the valley track.

11 ☐   Follow the track, steep in places, as far as the Musauer hut.

12 ☐   About $^1/_4$ mile (0.4km) beyond the hut, leave the track and turn right on a steep path which follows the river through the (Reintal) valley.

13 ☐   Cross the stream and rejoin the forest track a little further on.

14 ☐   Follow the track downhill for about $^1/_2$ mile (0.8km).

15 ☐   Turn left away from the track, steeply downhill through the last of the pine forest and out onto the flat valley bottom.

Lush meadows and bright sunshine of the valley contrast with the sometimes sombre confines deep within the forest.

16 ☐   Cross the meadow by following the red-white-red waymarks to join the main road close by a convenient restaurant and bus stop at Brandstatt about $4^1/_4$ miles (7km) north of Reutte.

E • THE AGGENSTEIN

---

7 miles (11km). 5–6 hours. Strenuous.

The Aggenstein marks the Austro-German border and as such it is a popular excursion with Bavarian mountain walkers, who can reach it either from Grän (as described in this walk), or from Pfronten in Germany. It is a real mountain in every sense. The Pfrontner hut, perched on a tiny ledge beneath the summit, is used by most visitors, either on the ascent or descent. The way up is steep and is protected by a wire rope; but it is the narrow rocky summit which really conveys the true feeling of being on high. The north side is sheer and on the south, the side used for this ascent, the slope is only marginally gentler.

Using the Füssener-Jöchli chairlift from Grän to reach 5,960ft (1,816m), the path turns north-west following the Tannheimer Höhenweg (high-level route) beneath a steep rocky ridge to the Pfrontner hut. A short but very steep rocky climb leads directly to the summit.

Returning as far as the hut, the route is southwards down the rock-strewn forested hillside to Enge and the Lumbergerhof Hotel. From here it is only a mile or so back to Grän.

The Route

1 □   Take the chairlift from Grän to the Füssener-Jöckli col.

Pause to admire the views on either side of the col. Even though you may have been this way before, the view changes with the light and time of day.

2 □   Turn left away from the upper station towards the north-west along a rocky path.

The path is steeper in places than the local map might suggest, so allow plenty of time for this section.

The ground around the old farm buildings below the Seebenspitze is often a riot of colourful alpine flowers. Marmots, large mountain rodents, may be seen or heard by their cheeky warning whistles along this section.

3 □   Walk on across a footpath junction and through the upper limits of the pine forest.

4 ☐   Climb the narrow path to the Pfrontner hut.

5 ☐   The final climb is obvious, but take care not to dislodge any stones. Also do not take short cuts. Use the wire rope as a handrail across the upper rocks.

Pause to admire the view. To the north is Bavaria and in the distance to the south, many of the Tyrolean giants jostle each other in a confusion of rock and ice.

6 ☐   Use the same route back down to the hut, again taking care on steep or loose sections.

7 ☐   Beyond the cross above the hut a path bears right. Take this, steeply downhill through the increasingly dense forest.

8 ☐   Cross a side stream, beyond which the descent eases a little.

Bird life is plentiful in the forest, as are small deer, but the shy creatures will only be seen by silent walkers.

9 ☐   The path joins a forest track and the gradient levels out above meadowland surrounding Enge.

10 ☐   Go left at a 'T' junction along a quiet side road, at the end of which will be found the Lumbergerhof Hotel and its friendly comfortable restaurant. A welcome end to a day spent on high.

11 ☐   The road from the hotel leads back to Grän.

Alpine gentians

F • NEUNERKOPF AND THE LANDSBURGER HUT

8 miles (13km). 5–6 hours. Strenuous.
2,731ft (832m) descent.

This is quite a hard walk, despite its apparently short distance. Even though the bulk of the route is along an almost level path, the sting is very much in the tail, for it is on the unrelentingly steep descent that the really hard part of the walk is found. Unfortunately this is at the end and could mar the day for anyone who had used up all their energy on the easy early stages. The advice is, take things easy, admire the views, but allow plenty of time for the climb down to Vilsalpsee from the Landsburger hut. Using both stages of the Neunerkopf chairlift to gain 2,573ft (784m), the route follows an easy, often level path to the Lachenjoch. This point marks the beginning of the difficult downhill section. At first, below the pass, the angle is moderate and the Landsburger hut on the far side of the Lache lake acts as a goal. Beyond the hut the path loses about 397ft (121m) in less than half a mile (0.8km) to the dam wall of the Traualpsee. It is, however, the last stage which is the steepest and hardest, from the reservoir down to Vilsalpsee 1,579ft (481m) are lost in less than $^3/_4$ mile (1.2km). So remember therefore, to keep some energy in reserve for this final stage.

The Route

1 ☐   Use both stages of the Neunerkopf chairlift from Tannheim village.

Pause to admire the view of the valley spread out below the Grund hut.

2 ☐   Follow the level waymarked path below the Vogelhorn ridge.

3 ☐   Ignore side paths and follow the contour round the rocky slopes of the Sulfspitz — 6,840ft (2,084m).

4 ☐   Walk down to the Gappenfeldscharte col.

The farmhouse to the right below the col sells refreshments.

5 ☐   Climb the rocky path to the side ridge below the Schochen-spitze — 6,856ft (2,089m).

The Schochenspitze's grassy summit makes an attractive short diversion away from the main path. The view is delightful, looking down on to the Vilstal .

Alpine flowers grow in abundance on the grassy ridge.

6 ☐   Walk downhill through low-growing scrubby pine, juniper trees and alpenrose, to the Lachenjoch.

The view of rocky Lachenspitze — 6,990ft (2,130m) beyond the tiny Lache lake with the colourful Landsburger hut in the foreground, will make all mountain photographers reach for their cameras.

7 ☐   Follow the lake shore and climb to the hut.

The Landsburger hut will make a good refreshment stop.

8 ☐   Follow the waymarked path down the steep rocky zigzags to the Traualpsee reservoir.

9 ☐   Beyond the dam wall, follow the clearly marked steep path down the winding trail into the forest.

10 ☐   Follow the stony bed of an old avalanche zone, roughly parallel to the side stream.

11 ☐   On reaching Vilsalpsee turn right along the level shore-side track. Follow it as far as the restaurants.

12 ☐   Follow the road away from Vilsalpsee.

13 ☐   Turn left on a side path and into the forest.

14 ☐   Rejoin the road. Turn left and follow it through the meadows to Tannheim.

G • THE ROTE FLUH

6 miles (9.6km). 4–5 hours. Strenuous.
3,200ft (975m) descent.

The Rote Fluh — 6,928ft (2,111m) — dominates the Tannheimertal skyline and is the goal of most of the climbers and mountain walkers who visit the valley. The route described here gains its initial height by the Hahnenkamm cable car followed by a rough walk across the lower slopes of the Kellespitze — 7,352ft (2,230m), to reach the Tannheim hut. At the hut a decision must be made — whether to attempt the final 1,283ft (391m) of steep scree and rock to reach the top of the Rote Fluh, or if weather and tiredness dictate otherwise, to walk down the steeply zigzagged path into Nesselwängle.

The final hundred feet or so to the top of the Rote Fluh includes a tricky section which involves climbing a short gully and crossing a sloping slab. The rock is, like the rest of the mountain, dolomitic limestone and the slab has been worn smooth by the boots of countless other climbers. In wet weather this short tricky section can be quite slippery and as it must be climbed down as well as up, it must be taken with great care. This section is not suitable for anyone with a poor head for heights. There is, however, a wire rope which will act as a handrail on the hardest part.

The Route

1 ☐   Either be driven by car (remember you do not return to the start point of this walk), or take the post bus over the Gaicht Pass to Höfen in the Lech valley. Most buses call at the Hahnenkamm cable car lower station, but enquire beforehand, otherwise it will mean a short uphill walk through the village of Höfen.

2 ☐   Take the Hahnenkamm cable car to its upper station.

The Hahnenkamm is a famous skiing area where top class competitions are held every winter.

There is an alpine garden run by the Austrian Alpine Flower Society above the Hahnenkamm slopes. The entrance is a little way beyond the cable car's upper station. Most of the alpine flowers found in the Austrian Alps are grown here in their natural setting, as well as rarer plants from the Himalayas and other mountain regions. Various sections of the garden explain the different environments in the mountains and how specialised plants have adapted themselves to these conditions.

3 ☐   Follow the waymarked path northwards, over the grassy Tief Joch.

4 ☐   Bear left downhill along a steep valley side to the Schneetalalpe farm.

Refreshments can be bought at the simple mountain farmhouse of Schneetalalpe.

5 ☐   Walk down into the next side valley.

6 ☐   Climb up through scrub pine and turn left at a path junction.

7 ☐   Follow the contours round the hillside to the Tannheim hut (refreshments available).

8 ☐   If climbing the Rote Fluh, follow the marked path steeply uphill on a scree slope to the right of the hut.

9 ☐   Bear left below a narrow gap in the ridge.

The mountain on the right is Gimpel—7,142ft (2,176m) — the domain of rock climbers who attempt the classic route of its western ridge.

10 ☐   Climb the Rote Fluh by way of the gully and slab, the former protected by a wire rope.

11 ☐   Admire the view from the summit and return the same way as on the upward route.

Take extra care on the descent, the rock is very smooth.

12 ☐   Climb down the steep path to the Gimpelhaus hut.

13 ☐   Follow the zigzags steeply down through the forest into Nesselwängle village.

H • UNTERJOCH

11 miles (18km). 3–4 hours. Easy.

The border between Germany and Austria crosses a low stretch of moorland at the lower end of the valley. The river turns north at this point and breaks through a gap in the ridge before descending to the Bavarian plain near Pfronten.

This walk follows the valley downstream from Tannheim past quiet villages and into the frontier forest, calling at the Rehbach hut on the way. The border follows no easily recognised geographical features above Rehbach and only the observant are likely to see occasional square concrete blocks at ground level by the side of the footpath. These mark the actual border.

Unterjoch is in Germany and even though it is only $1^1/_2$ miles (2.4km) from Austria the general ambience of the place is definitely German.

The return to Austria is along a quiet lane where the border is marked by a tiny customs post. Manning it must be one of the most pleasant jobs in customs service. It is unlikely that walkers will be asked to show their passports, but to be on the safe side, it is recommended that they are carried.

The Route

1 □   Start in Tannheim village and follow the side road to Berg. Go under the bypass.

2 □   Turn left through the hamlet of Berg to follow the level metalled lane through meadowland to Untergschwend and Zöblen.

The little wayside chapel dedicated to St Leonhard between Berg and Untergschwend is worth visiting.

3 □   Follow the lane as far as the main road. Turn right and almost immediately right again on a side road following the river.

4 □   Keeping above and to the right of the river, walk past the scattered farms and villas of Schattwald.

5 □   The metalled lane becomes an unsurfaced track. Follow it into the forest.

6 ☐   The track climbs a little to pass a rocky outcrop hidden further down the slope on the left.

7 ☐   Descend steeply to the river and bear left, then steeply uphill to the hospitable *Gasthof* at Rehbach.

8 ☐   Walk away to the left from Rehbach. Go round the steep hairpin bend.

9 ☐   At the top of the rise beyond the bend, a path on the right of the road leads steeply uphill over meadowland into Germany.

10 ☐   Left along the tree-lined lane and right at a road junction. Walk down this road into Unterjoch.

Unterjoch, a quiet rural village, has a couple of restaurants and old farm buildings, but the church is the most interesting feature, especially its ultra-modern interior architecture.

11 ☐   Walk back along the road to the first junction and turn right.

12 ☐   Follow the road to Krumbach. Turn left by field path to the border road at In der Bränte.

13 ☐   Turn right along the road, cross the border and walk down into the Vils valley.

14 ☐   Go past a timber yard and join the main road by the side of the restaurant opposite the Austrian customs post.

A regular bus service runs along the valley back to Tannheim, although the walk could be extended using paths and tracks to the south of the main road.

2 DAMÜLS

Map _____

Kompass Wanderkarte (1:50,000 series) Sheet 2; Bregenzer Wald-Westallgäu.

How to Get There

Road

1 • South by the European motorway system to Basel, then east via Zurich and St Gallen into Austria. Follow the A14 south to Rankweil. Damüls is to the east by minor road across the Furka Pass.

2 • Via the Black Forest and the north shore of Lake Constance (Bodensee) to Bregenz and Dornbirn. South-east on road 200 to Au, the Hochtannen-Bergerstrasse; Damüls is to the south-west along a single track road.

Note: There may be a variable direction flow system in operation on this narrow single track road. Check the times carefully on schedules displayed at the start of restricted sections.

Rail

Main line services by the Arlberg Express to Dornbirn followed by post bus over the Furka Pass.

Air

Nearest international airport is Zurich. Rail to Dornbirn then post bus.

The Area

Unlike the Austrian alpine giants further east, the mountains of Bregenzer Wald are made of shale and so are mostly grass covered. They offer an entirely different kind of walking to that normally experienced in the higher mountains. Grassy tracks lead easily along terraces beneath rounded summits whose heights rarely go above 6,500ft (2,000m) Many of the high-level paths can be reached by the Uga chairlift which climbs from the Hohes Licht to Eisenalpstube, then by a second stage to the Damüls Mittagspitz col. Using the lift will avoid approximately 2,300ft (700m) of fairly steep climbing. The only drawback to walking on grassy slopes is that they can be slippery after rain, otherwise they are ideal for easy, high-level rambling.

Damüls village follows the line of its single street and was originally a staging post on the one-time important east-west road across the Furka Pass—5,776ft (1,760m). Few links remain from the old coaching days and even though many of the hotels retain something of their earlier simplicity, most of the older buildings have been swamped beneath modern extensions. It is perhaps the church which keeps any links with bygone days. Its 'onion' dome topping the bell tower and steeply pitched roof, has guided travellers along an often hazardous road for centuries. Attractive murals decorate its interior walls and the baroque splendour of its gilded altar makes the church an architectural gem.

Damüls is undoubtably more popular in winter than in summer, but this gives it an edge over the more traditional mountain walking areas of Austria. Here is a peaceful haven where the air has a relaxed feel; but not too much to deter the visitor from exploring the grassy hillsides and ridges of the surrounding peaks and their valleys.

Flower lovers will enjoy this region; the sheltered hillsides are covered in alpine flowers of almost every variety.

Easy road access makes Damüls an excellent centre for touring in the Bregenzer Wald and other parts of Austria or even eastern Switzerland.The latter is only a handful of miles away, across the deep rift of the Rhine valley. Lichtenstein is even closer, geographically part of Austria, but politically linked to Switzerland. Lake cruises to inland ports in both Germany and Switzerland are a popular rest day excursion from nearby Bregenz. Bregenz itself is an interesting place, the major town in the region, it hosts a cultural festival every year from mid-July to mid-August, when visiting operatic and ballet companies stage performances.

The textile fair in nearby Dornbirn is now an important annual event, rivalling Paris with its fashion shows.

Useful Information

Local Tourist Office
Verkehrsamt Damüls
A.6884 Damüls
☎ 5510/253

Accommodation

Regional Tourist Office
Landesverkehrsamt Vorarlberg
Römerstrasse 77/1
A6901 Bregenz
☎ (5574) 22525-0

Ranges from three-and four-star hotels to guest-houses and rented accommodation. Nearest camp site at Raggal—7 miles (11km) south-west of Damüls.

Cable Cars and Chairlifts in the Area

Damüls   Uga two-stage chairlift from Hoheslicht
Dornbirn   Karren cable car from Oberdorf
Bludenz   Muttersberg cable car
Bregenz   Pfänder cable car
Schoppernau   Diedamskopf two-stage chairlift
Bezau   Baumgarten cable car from Oberbezau

Recommended Local Excursions

Bludenz 25 miles (40km) south over the Furka Pass. Old town, shops, restaurants, cable car.

Bregenz 28 miles (45km) north-north-west. Lakeside town, regional capital, Roman remains, music festival, casino, shops, deer park, cable car.

Dornbirn 23 miles (37km) north-west over the Furka Pass. Textile centre, annual trade fair, music festival, cable car.

Feldkirch 14 miles (22km) south-west over the Furka Pass. Parts date from the Middle Ages. Shopping arcades. Schattenberg Castle.

Lindau (Germany) 33 miles (53km) north-west. Lakeside resort.

Lake cruises Regular cruises from Bregenz to German and Swiss towns on the shores of Lake Constance (Bodensee). **Note:** If you plan to leave the ferry at any of the German or Swiss resorts, remember to take passports and local currency.

Bregenz makes an interesting excursion from Damüls

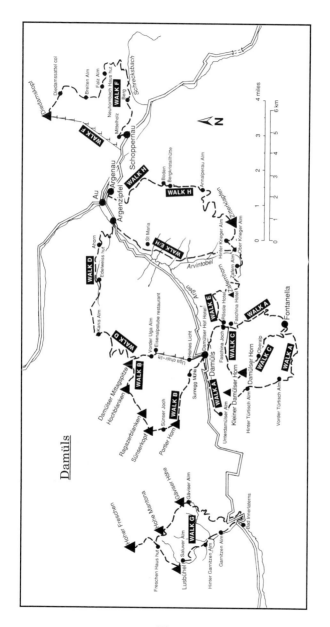

Damüls

WALK F
Diedamskopf
Diedamssattel col
Breiten Alm
Falz Alm
Neuhornbach Haus hut
WALK F
Berg
Mittelholz
Schreckisbach
WALK F

Au
Argenau
Argenzipfel
Schoppernau
WALK H
Boden
Bergkristallhütte
Annalpenau Alm
WALK H
Zitterklapfen
Hinter Krieger Alm
Ober Krieger Alm
Zaferm Alm
Zafernhorn

WALK D
Ahorn
Edelweiss hut
WALK E/H
St Maria
Arvintobel
Argen

Karls Alm
WALK D
Vorder Uga Alm
Eisenalpstube restaurant
WALK E
Rössle Hotel
Faschina Hotel
WALK A
Fontanella
WALK C
Oberalp
WALK A
Vorder Türtsch Alm

WALK B
Damüser Mittagspitze
Hochblanken
Ragazerblanken
Sunserkopf
Sunser Joch
WALK B
Portler Horn
Uga chair-lift
Hohes Licht
Surneg Mähe
Damüls
Damülser Hof Hotel
Faschina Joch
WALK A
Unterdamüser Alm
Kleiner Damülser Horn
WALK C
Damülser Horn
Hinter Türtsch Alm

Hoher Freschen
Freschen Haus hut
Hohe Matona
Lusbühel
Saluver Alm
Saluver Alm
Saluver Höhe
WALK G
Hinter Gamtzen Alm
Gamtzen Alm
Bad Innerlaterns

N

4 miles
6 km

37

A • AROUND THE DAMÜLSER HORN

9¹/₄ miles (15km). 5–6 hours. Easy.

Here is a pleasant walk with very little climbing, an easy start to a walking holiday in Damüls. The only climb of any note is at the beginning of the walk, but even this is gradual. A farm track climbs steadily away from the western end of the village, along the Argenbach valley to the hill farmsteads of Unterdamülser Alm. From here the route is round the steep north-western spur of the Damülser Horn (also known as the Glatthorn)—7,004ft (2,134m), one of the dominant peaks in the area and a possible climb later in the holiday. Turning east, the way leads directly to the village of Fontanella and its inviting *Gasthöfe*, ideal for a late lunch stop or afternoon's refreshment break. An easy road climbs to the low col of Faschina Joch and down across the 'home' valley into Damüls.

This walk is also suitable for a rainy day as much of the route is along forest tracks and paths. Open meadows surrounding farmsteads are in marked contrast, especially in early summer when they are filled with a blaze of colourful alpine flowers such as blue monkshood and sulphur-yellow anemones.

The Route

1 ☐   Walk up the main road away from the centre of the village, as far as the first hairpin bend. Turn left on a farm track.

2 ☐   Follow the track, above the Argenbach, through meadows and past barns and occasional farm houses.

The south-facing hillsides above the Argenbach can be a riot of colour until haymaking time. The hay is stored in the ancient timber barns which are built almost at random on the sloping meadowland.

3 ☐   At the old farmhouse of Unterdamülser Alm take the furthest left path at the signpost.

4 ☐   Climb steadily around the sparsely wooded slopes of the Kleiner Damülser Horn, the north-western spur of the Damülser Horn.

5 ☐   The climb ends at Hinter Türtisch Alm, where the path gently descends over rocky ground to the group of farm buildings of Vorder Türtisch Alm.

On the Damülser Horn

6 □   Go through a small section of pine forest and bear left around the southern spur of the mountain.

The deep-cut valley on the right is the Ladritscher, known locally by its old dialect name of the Ladritschtobel.

7 □   Walk downhill and join a hillside road at the bottom of a ski-tow.

8 □   Turn left along the road, following its level course into the tiny village of Fontanella.

Fontanella is a delightful little village with one or two Gasthöfe *and an interesting church.*

9 □   Start to walk down into the Faschina valley.

10 □   Turn left at a junction with the valley road and follow it beneath the spreading boughs of mature pines to the col at Faschina Joch.

Refreshments are available at Faschina Joch.

11 □   Bear left, downhill, across the Argenbach valley.

12 □   Use the signposted path to avoid road walking and climb back to Damüls, entering the village close by the village store.

B • THE DAMÜLSER MITTAGSPITZE

6¹/₄ miles (10km). 5–6 hours. Moderate.
1,971ft (602m) descent.

The steep initial climb on this walk is avoided by using the first stage of the Uga chairlift as far as the Eisenalpstube restaurant. Easy, but steep climbing follows the skyline ridges of the Damülser Mittagspitze, Hochblanken and Ragazerblanken. Leaving the ridge at the Portler Horn, the route steadily traverses across a hillside more popular in winter when skiers crowd its open slopes.

The summit of the Damülser Mittagspitze—6,876ft (2,095m) is the scene of an annual pilgrimage. The local bishop, in all his robes, holds a mass beneath the massive cross which marks the top of this conspicuous mountain. This act of devotion is not without its hazards, as high winds which blow across the summit, often threaten to lift the bishop. The major task for his acolytes is to hold him down on such occasions!

As the path is narrow and can be muddy after rain, the walk is not recommended in wet weather, although a safer alternative does exist (see below). The safer path crosses the upper combe of the Krumbach to avoid the steepest slopes.

The Route

1 ☐   Take the Uga chairlift from the Hohes Licht to the Eisenalpstube restaurant.

The ride is a pleasant introduction to the walk. The almost silent cable climbs steadily at tree-top height above the valley to reach the welcoming restaurant.

2 ☐   Turn left away from the top station and follow the access track as far as a group of farm buildings at Vorder Uga Alm.

3 ☐   Take the central of three paths, away from the track, and climb towards the col on the right of the prominent slopes of the Damülser Mittagspitze.

In wet weather, or for anyone without a head for heights, it is recommended that the path which turns left beneath the lowest part of the second stage of the Uga ski-tow cable, be followed. This

crosses a wide combe in the upper Krumbach valley and rejoins the
main ridge on less steep slopes to the north-east of Ragazerblanken.

4 ☐　Turn left at the col, steeply uphill following the narrow path to the summit of the Damülser Mittagspitze — 6,876ft (2,095m).

Pause beneath the summit cross to admire the wide-ranging views
of the Bregenzer Wald and also both the Austrian and Swiss Alps
further afield.

5 ☐　Walk downhill with care, to a dip in the ridge. Go under a chair-lift cable and climb Hochblanken — 6,787ft (2,068m).

6 ☐　Follow the grassy ridge on safer slopes to Ragazerblanken — 6,731ft (2,051m).

Shales which form the characteristic slopes of the hills to the north and
east of Ragazerblanken, give way to harder rock. The south-eastern
slope is fairly gentle and grassy, but the north-westerly face is more
open and craggy. Take care not to stray to this side of the ridge.

7 ☐　Climb Sunserkopf — 6,669ft (2,032m) and bear left to the south along the broad grassy ridge.

8 ☐　Cross the Sunser Joch and make the final climb to the Portler Horn — 6,597ft (2,010m).

9 ☐　Bear left downhill over the stony hillside.

10 ☐　Turn left at a path junction, following the broad spur downhill to the Sunnegg *Gasthof.*

11 ☐　Follow the access drive down to the main road.

12 ☐　Turn left, past the Damülser Hof Hotel, and walk down the road back into Damüls.

C • THE DAMÜLSER HORN (GLATTHORN)

8¹/₂ miles (14km). 6–7 hours. Moderate.
2,127ft (648m) ascent.

This attractive mountain is a popular climb from either Damüls or the more remote village of Fontanella. Both are visited no matter which way the walk is followed, and in their own charming way, try to waylay the hillwalker into a delayed start to the walk.

A short but useful chairlift avoids the steep climb from Faschina Joch. A narrow grassy ridge with a clear path leads directly from the top station, towards the summit of the Damülser Horn.

Turning south, then south-east, the downhill path is steep at first then uses easier slopes directly into Fontanella. A forest road takes the walker back across the Faschina Joch, road walking which can be avoided by the use of the local bus service.

The Route

1 ☐   From the general store walk downhill out of Damüls by the cross valley path. Join the new road on the far side.

2 ☐   Climb the broad col of Faschina Joch.

3 ☐   Turn right away from the road by the side of the Faschina Hotel. Use either the chairlift or follow the path steeply uphill.

4 ☐   Follow the path above the upper chairlift station, away from the sparse pine trees, up the steadily narrowing grassy ridge.

5 ☐   Scramble over easy rocks to the summit of the Damülser Horn — 7,004ft (2,134m).

The view to the south takes in the Raitikon range across the deep trough of the Grosser Walsertal. The Silvretta range marking the border with Switzerland lies further to the south-east. The Swiss canton of St Gallen marks the western view across the Rhine valley.

6 ☐   Ignore the first path off to the left, but follow the ridge southwards to a rocky col.

7 ☐   Turn left downhill over rocky ground, then bear right onto open

Fontanella

alpine pasture and a group of farm buildings at Oberalp.

8 □   Continue to walk downhill to Fontanella.

9 □   Keep left at a fork, into forest, and go down steeply to a forest track.

10 □   Turn right at a 'T' junction and walk down to the village of Fontanella.

Pause for refreshments in Fontanella and admire the interesting architecture of this alpine village (see also the Kanis Alm walk).

It may be possible to catch a bus and avoid the road walk back to Faschina Joch, otherwise:

11 □   Turn left along the road, following it back uphill to Faschina Joch.

12 □   Cross the col and avoid the road by using the side path to reach Damüls on the opposite side of the valley.

D • KANIS ALM AND THE EDELWEISS HUT

$7\frac{1}{2}$ miles (12km). 6–7 hours. Moderate.

The atmosphere of a mountain hut is something which cannot be experienced anywhere other than in remote high-level places. Their special ambience cannot be explained to those who are not mountain lovers. The friendly, easy-going, relaxed way of life is one thing, but overall there is a certain something which all true lovers of the mountains will understand.

The Edelweiss hut is visited on this walk, a typical mountain retreat, a special favourite of the author, who once found it in a dense fog purely by the aroma of coffee which drifted along the shrouded mountainside. The coffee lived up to its expectations, complemented by a massive portion of the lightest chocolate cake imaginable.

Using the first stage of the Uga chairlift to gain most of the height, the route crosses the col below the Damülser Mittagspitze, then wanders idly over an open hillside to reach a side col above Kanis Alm. Careful navigation is required to gain the Leue valley and the Edelweiss hut. (Remember that the coffee pot may not always be bubbling away to guide travellers.) A roughly surfaced road below the hut leads into the main valley where it is a short ride back to Damüls.

The Route

1 □   Take the Uga chairlift to the Eisenalpstube restaurant.

2 □   Turn left, away from the top station, along the service track towards a group of farm buildings at Vorder Uga Alm.

3 □   Turn right uphill on a well defined path, aiming for the grassy col on the east side of steep Damülser Mittagspitze.

The view northwards is over the rolling grassy mountains of the Bregenzerwald, all easy walking country. In the distance the central German plain is to the right and away on the left, showing as hazy upland, lies the Black Forest.

4 □   Walk on downhill over the stony hillsides and follow a path to the right around the headwaters of the Alpbach.

5 □   Turn right at a path junction beyond Kanis Alm, a ruined farm .

6 ☐ Fork right and climb along forest paths over a broad col.

7 ☐ Continue along the path, downhill on the gradually improving surface of a track.

8 ☐ Reach the Edelweiss hut and pause for refreshment.

9 ☐ Bear left, downhill from the hut and into the headwaters of the Leue Bach.

10 ☐ Climb above the river, following a slanting path through the forest.

11 ☐ Walk down to the hillside hamlet of Ahorn.

The rocky mountain due south, is Zitterklapfen — 7,887ft (2,403m).

12 ☐ Follow the access track, zigzagging downhill into the main valley to Argenzipfel.

13 ☐ Catch the post bus back up the valley unless you are able to make alternative travel arrangements.

E • THE ZAFERNHORN

$8^1/_2$ miles (14km). 7–8 hours. Moderate/Strenuous.

The Zafernhorn — 6,915ft (2,107m) rises to the east of Faschina Pass, almost the twin of the Damülser Horn in the west. The climb to reach it is steep and the path climbs steadily across the forested northern slope of the Zafernhorn, before reaching a narrow col below its east face. A short but stiff pull is required to reach the summit. Returning to the col, a side path drops down into the Arvintobel valley where care must be taken to keep to the correct route and avoid tempting, but wrong side paths. Following the path, and later a forest road beneath the shade of pine trees, the route leads into the main valley reaching the road at Argenzipfel.

The Route

1 ☐ Cross the valley below Damüls and climb to the pass at Faschina Joch.

An early coffee can be bought at one of the restaurants on the pass, the only opportunity for bought refreshment this side of Argenzipfel.

2 ☐   Take the path on the left of the Rössle Hotel and climb across the steep meadow towards the forest edge.

3 ☐   Pass through belts of mature forest and cross alpine meadows, passing a wayside shrine on the way.

4 ☐   Turn right uphill at a footpath junction.

5 ☐   Bear right at the next junction.

6 ☐   Climb the easing angle of the rocky slope, crossing the eastern arm of the Zafernhorn on the way.

7 ☐   Go through the narrow col and bear slightly right to a footpath 'cross roads'.

8 ☐   Turn right steeply uphill to the summit of Zafernhorn.

9 ☐   Admire the view from the summit and return by the same route.

10 ☐   Cross the outward path and walk gently downhill to a group of farm buildings at Zafern Alm.

Zafern Alm is only used occasionally during the summer months by farmers who bring animals to the high pasture, from the main farms in the valleys below Fontanella and Damüls.

11 ☐   Cross the side valley and climb to a path which leads through meadows above the right-hand side of the Arvintobel river.

12 ☐   Bear left into forest at a path junction and walk down to Hinter Krieger Alm.

13 ☐   Cross an open meadow into dense pine forest.

14 ☐   Join a forest track and bear right downhill crossing side streams by rustic bridges.

15 ☐   Do not leave the track when you reach open meadowland below the hamlet of St Maria on top of a prominent rise.

16 ☐   Turn left at a track junction below the hamlet and follow an improving road into the main valley.

17 ☐   Walk through forest above the River Argen, steadily downhill to the open farmland surrounding Argenzipfel, and return by post bus.

F • DIEDAMSKOPF

$5^1/_2$ miles (9km). 5–6 hours. Moderate.
4,070ft (1,240m) descent.

By using the Diedamskopf chairlift above Schoppernau on the Warth to Dornbirn road, this walk becomes mainly one of descent. With one or two minor exceptions such as the gentle slope up to the Neuhornbach Haus hut, the way is downhill from start to finish.

From the top of the Diedamskopf the route follows well defined and waymarked footpaths, at first in a zone of scrub pines and juniper bushes. These give way later to taller trees the closer one gets to the main valley. Open hillsides dotted with alpine flowers are crossed to reach the hospitality of the Neuhornbach Haus hut, a well sited hospice with a breathtaking view across the Bregenzer Ache valley. Beyond the hut, the path improves until it becomes a jeep track and this is used to reach Schoppernau, the start and finish of the walk.

The Route

1 ☐ Drive or take the post bus from Damüls via Au to Schoppernau and use the chair-lift to the Diedamskopf summit— 6,859ft (2,090m).

To the north and east lie the last outliers of the Austrian mountains, marking the border with Germany. Southwards is the Inn valley and beyond it the Silvretta range and the Austrian/Switss border.

2 ☐ Follow the footpath along the south-east ridge of Diedamskopf, downhill through scrubby pine and well to the right of the craggy edge.

3 ☐ Ignore a path on the right, (direct route to Schoppernau).

4 ☐ Take the first of three paths all joining on Diedamssattel col.

5 ☐ Turn right from the col, downhill over an open hillside.

6 ☐ Bear left at a path junction by the old farmhouse of Breiten Alm.

7 ☐ Follow the shoulder of the hillside, downhill to the left, skirting patchy forest.

8 ☐ Walk ahead at Falz Alm and follow the contours round the hillside. Cross a small stream.

9 ☐ Climb slightly to reach the Neuhornbach Haus hut.

The view across the valley is directly onto the Zitterklapfen range and its rocky satellites. Damüls is to the right at the head of the Argenbach valley and just out of sight, screened by the shoulder of Annalper Stecken, the north ridge of Zitterklapfen.

10 □   Walk steeply downhill to the south away from the hut. Zigzag through forest towards the Schrecksbach stream.

11 □   Turn right at a path junction and walk downstream on an easier path.

12 □   Cross a side stream and turn right, uphill to the old farm at Berg.

13 □   Downhill to the jeep road serving the Neuhornbach Haus hut.

14 □   Turn left and follow the track, across the slope of the hill towards a group of farm buildings and holiday cottages at Mittelholz.

15 □   Left at the junction on a surfaced road into the centre of Schoppernau.

G • HOHER FRESCHEN

9¹/₂ miles (15km). 8 hours. Strenuous.
2,813ft (857m) ascent.

If the previous walk was an entirely downhill affair, then this, the ascent of Hoher Freschen — 6,577ft (2,004m), is very much in the order of a mountain climb, though it is a fairly straightforward one. The steepest part of the 2,813ft (857m) involved in the ascent is in the early stages on a track which zigzags carefully up the mountain.

The climb follows all the rules of interesting mountaineering; in other words it is not one boring straight up or down, but follows first one ridge then crosses a high combe to reach the final sharp pull below the rocky summit.

The route starts at the roadside about 1³/₄ miles (2.8 km) below the Furka Joch Pass west of Damüls, then climbs beyond the tree line to the remote farmsteads at Gäviser Alm. On open ground it follows a rocky ridge to the satellite peak of Hohe Mantona. Finally it crosses a high combe passing a well sited mountain hut and on to the summit. Returning to the hut, the descent is by way of the Garnitzen Bach.

As there are a number of side paths which could be misleading, this climb should only be attempted in clear weather.

The Route

1 ☐ Start from the roadside restaurant at Bad Innerlaterns. Walk up the Damüls road and follow it beyond the bridge as far as the second hairpin.

2 ☐ Turn left on the farm track, zigzag uphill to Gäviser Alm.

The track winds in and out of forest towards the open alpine meadows surrounding Gäviser Alm.

3 ☐ Go left uphill towards a prominent rise marked with a cross. This is Gäviser Hohe — 5,868ft (1,788m).

4 ☐ Follow the broad ridge to Hohe Mantona — 6,554ft (1,997m).

5 ☐ Go slightly downhill across the intervening rocky combe to the Freschen Haus hut.

6 ☐ Turn right at the hut, uphill to the rocky summit of Hoher Freschen — 6,577ft (2,004m).

Pause to admire the view and compliment yourself on achieving the summit. Take care on the descent, steep ground is more difficult and hazardous when descending.

7 ☐ Return to the hut and turn right.

8 ☐ Go downhill beneath the gradually narrowing ridge to a cross which marks the start of easier ground. This is Lusbühel.

9 ☐ Turn left at the cross, downhill and cross the stream to reach a group of farm buildings at Unter Saluver Alm.

The sheltered alp is often full of alpine flowers, alpenrose will be found blooming from late June to July.

10 ☐ Join a jeep track at Hinter Garnitzen Alm and follow it along the left bank of the Garnitzen Bach.

11 ☐ Go past the bottom stations of two supply cables serving the upper farms and walk down to the main road.

12 ☐ Turn right along the road for about $1/4$ mile (402m) to reach Bad Innerlaterns.

H • ZITTERKLAPFEN

$10^1/_2$ miles (17km). 7–8 hours. Strenuous.
4,815ft (1,467m) ascent.

This is the toughest walk in the neighbourhood of Damüls, the climb is long and steep and not without its technical difficulties. The walk is not suitable for the poorly equipped, or anyone without a good head for heights.

Starting and finishing in the village of Au, the route goes first through Argenzipfel, then along the Argen valley and up the Arventobel tributary to Hinter Krieger Alm. Left here and steeply to the summit. The return is along the narrow north ridge and then zigzags down its broad shoulder into the Dürren valley. A forest track leads out of the valley and so down to Au.

This is a long hard walk and plenty of time must be allowed for its completion.

The Route

1 □   Either take the post bus to Argenzipfel, or from Au walk back along the Damüls road, through Argenzipfel almost as far as the road bridge.

Au is an important route centre at the junction of the Bregenzer and Argen valleys. It is the main town for the surrounding villages, offering shops to supply most local needs.

2 □   Turn left along the lane and climb through forest towards open fields below St Maria.

3 □   Bear right at the junction below St Maria. Climb steadily in and out of shady patches of forest and into the Arvintobel valley.

4 □   Where the track turns sharply right and drops down to the stream, walk forwards at a bend onto the woodland footpath.

5 □   Climb as far as the old farm at Hinter Krieger Alm.

6 □   Turn sharp left, steeply uphill across alpine meadows to Ober Krieger Alm and swing right across the mountainside.

7 □   After about $^1/_4$ mile (402m) there is a signposted path on the left. Follow this steep path to the rocky summit of Zitterklapfen.

Zitterklapfen — 7,411ft (2,258m) is the highest peak in the locality of Damüls and is an excellent vantage point. Photographers will enjoy the opportunity to take shots of the wide-ranging views.

8 □ Follow the waymarking red-white paint splashes along the rocky and narrow north-east ridge. Cross several minor summits.

Take extra care on this ridge, especially when descending towards less steep ground.

9 □ Bear sharp right at point 2124, below the broken ground of the eastern side arm of the ridge.

10 □ Swing left above a line of crags onto easier ground and follow a winding path.

11 □ Turn right at the junction, downhill towards the Dürren valley and back into forest.

12 □ Follow the left bank of the Dürren, past the farm buildings at Annalperau Alm.

13 □ Call at the Bergkristallhütte for refreshment.

14 □ Go through Boden, cross the side stream and take the left of two paths.

15 □ Follow this around the forested hillside, over one stream then right at the next on an improving track.

16 □ Walk down into Argenau.

17 □ Turn left along the road for about $1/2$ mile (804m) to reach Au, tired but proud of your achievement in climbing the Zitterklapfen.

3 OETZ

Map
Kompass Wanderkarte (1:50,000 series) Sheet 35; Imst-Telfs-
Kühtai.

How to Get There

Road
1 • European motorway system east to Ulm, then south via Kempten,
Ehrwald and the Fern Pass to Imst. Oetz is to the south-east across
the Inn valley.
2 • South to Basel, then east via Zurich and Lake Constance
(Bodensee) to the Arlburg Pass or tunnel. Follow the Inn valley
beyond Landeck and Imst to the Oetz turning.

Rail
1 • Trans-European system — the Arlberg Express — to the nearest
stopping station, then local service to Bahnstation Ötztal. The village
of Oetz is a short taxi ride away — about $3^1/_2$ miles (6km).
2 • Via Munich and Innsbruck and local train to Oetz.

Air
International Airports situated at Innsbruck and Munich. Connections
by rail as **2** above.

The Area

Oetz is situated at the mouth of the Ötztal valley which drains
northwards from the Ötztaler Alpen, one of the chain of peaks marking
the Austro-Italian border. These peaks are beyond the capabilities of
most hillwalkers, but can still be appreciated from vantage points near
the head of the valley above Vent or Obergurgl. The highest points on
the border ridge are marked by the graceful snowy beauty of the
Weisskugel — 12,271ft (3,739m) and Similaun — 11,838ft (3,607m);
with the Wildspitze — 12,367ft (3,768m) a little to the north of the main
range and in fact the highest peak in the area. All-year-round skiing
takes place on the slopes of many of the surrounding peaks. There is
a high-level road, the Timmels-Joch, leading over the border at an
altitude of 8,120ft (2,474m), into the Passer valley of northern Italy.
This road is above Agern, high in the Ötztal valley and could be used

to explore some of the easier sections of the border ridges.

Walking in the Ötztal is distinctly divided between mountain rambling and serious mountaineering expeditions. This guide is restricted to the former and, therefore, the walks are concentrated on the lower part of the valley around the village of Oetz.The areas above Vent and Obergurgl are, however, highly recommended for anyone with a taste for adventure and who may want to explore the peaks and glaciers of the upper valley. A series of mountain huts, strategically placed, offer overnight accommodation for mountaineers wanting to climb in the Ötztal and Stubai Alps.

Around Oetz the walking is mostly along forested hillsides, ideal for hot summer days. One chairlift serves the eastern arm of the lower valley making possible several high-level routes above the tree line. As the valley is narrow, walking in it is restricted to lanes and farm tracks taking in many of the old hamlets and farmsteads now bypassed by the more up-to-date motor road. Short lengths of path on either bank of the River Inn can be linked to make several walks along this major European waterway.

The Ötztal valley has a range of widely differing activities and festivals throughout the summer months. Flocks of sheep are taken into the mountains in June and brought back about mid-September, depending upon the weather. Organised walks, some to nearby glaciers, are available throughout the valley; check with the local tourist information bureau for details. Obergurgl has a music work-shop at the end of July, under the Suzuki method of teaching. Perhaps the best time of all is at the end of June, when the valley is a blaze of purples and reds of the alpenrose bushes which cover many of the nearby hillsides between the tree line and snow. All-year-round skiing instruction is available from Obergurgl.

Oetz village is a quiet retreat, but it has everything a mountain holidaymaker requires, from a naturally heated swimming pool to tennis and keep-fit courses. The local tourist office gives details of the walking badge scheme for the district.

Useful Information

Local Tourist Office
Tiroler Landesreisbüro — Verkehrsbüro Oetz
c/o Fremdenverkehrsverband Oetz
Postfach 2
A6433 Oetz/Tirol   ☎ 052 52/66 69

Church at Vent, near Sölden in the Ötztal

Accommodation
Mostly *Gasthöfe*, *pensions*, bed and breakfast and rented cottages, but also a number of first-rate family run hotels. One camp site but several others nearby.

Chairlift
The Acher Kogelbahn chairlift climbs towards the Rotes Wandl from the south end of the village close to the swimming pool. There are others further up the valley, some of which give suitable access to year-round skiing areas.

Recommended Excursions
Innsbruck   Famous historical city, museums. Access to Karwendel mountains.

Seefeld   Busy mountain town near the German border. Shops, restaurants, forest walks, large indoor swimming pool.

Timmels Joch   High-level motor road — 8,120ft (2,474m) — into Italy from the Ötztal valley. Check snow conditions before attempting the journey.

Zugspitze   Germany's highest mountain 9,718ft (2,962m) on Austrian border. Access by cable car from Ehzwald, the Tiroler Zugspitzbahn. Glacier walks, viewpoint, restaurant and summer skiing.

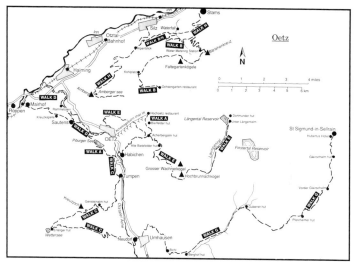

Stams

Silz Waterfall
Ötztal-
Bahnhof
WALK B/H
WALK H

Oetz

Alpenblick
Water Metering Station
Bärenfalenkreuz

Haiming
Kohlplatz
Faltegartenkögele
WALK H

N

0   1   2   3   4 miles
0   1 2 3 4 5 6 km

Amberg
WALK H
Amberger see
Ochsengarten restaurant
WALK B

WALK D
Mairhof
Hochoetz restaurant
Dortmunder hut
Längental Reservoir
St Sigmund-in-Sellrain

Roppen
Kreuzkapelle
Rammelstein
WALK E
Bielfelder hut
Unter Längentalm
Hubertus Hotel

Sautens
WALK D
Acherbergalm hut
Finstertal Reservoir
Gleirschalm hut

Pburger See
OETZ
Alte Bielefelder hut
WALK E
Habichen
WALK A
Vorder Gleirschalm

WALK G
Grosser Wachnerkogel
WALK G
Hochbrunnachkogel
Tumpen

Kreuzjoch
Gamsteinalpe hut
Juifener hut
Pforzheimer hut

WALK C
WALK C
Erlanger hut
Wettersee
Neudorf
Umhausen
WALK G
Bichl
Berghof hut

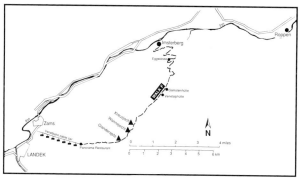

Inn
Roppen
Imsterberg
Eggewiesse

WALK F
Gamsteinhütte
Venetaphütte

Kreuzjoch
Wannejoch
Glanderspitz

Zams
Venetbahn cable car
N

0   1   2   3   4 miles
0   1 2 3 4 5 6 km

LANDEK
Panorama Restaurant

55

A • ROTES WANDL

$4^1/_2$ miles (7km). 2 hours. Easy.

Anyone visiting the Ötztal for the first time will certainly want to know as much as possible about the surrounding area. No doubt visitors will have read everything they can in advance of the holiday, but there is nothing better than climbing to a vantage point with map in hand, to identify the surrounding features.

This first walk fulfills just such a function. By using the Acherkogel-bahn chairlift, the walk starts on a delightful vantage point, also served by a restaurant. Its veranda is an ideal place from which to look along the Ötztal valley towards the high peaks and glaciers of the Ötztaler Alps. In the other direction, the view is across the deep trough of the Inn valley towards the serried ranks of the Lechtal range and its rocky satellites.

The walk away from the chairlift is downhill through forest, on an easy path which follows the gradient by carefully engineered zigzags. The route goes through Habichen village and across the valley road, then climbs a low wooded hill, to reach the Piburger See where an easy road leads back to Oetz.

The Route

1 ☐ Take both stages of the Acherkogelbahn chairlift from its bottom station, near the sports centre, to the Hochoetz restaurant — 6,630ft (2,020m).

Pause for awhile to admire the view from the restaurant and try to identify the surrounding peaks — a map is essential.

2 ☐ Follow the service road south and away from the restaurant.

3 ☐ Turn left after about 200yd (180m), at a signpost pointing towards the Bielefelder hut. Follow the path.

4 ☐ Go downhill following the footpath sign to the Acherbergalm hut. Alpenrose bushes dot the hillsides away from the confining pine forest.

5 ☐ Follow the zigzag route of the path, downhill through dense pine forest. Keep right at path junctions.

A stop for refreshments on the Acherberger Alm

Stations of the Cross mark the lower path, a feature of most alpine countries.

6 ☐ Bear left into a lane and follow it down to Habichen.

7 ☐ Go left through the village and cross the valley road and the river.

8 ☐ Bear right away from the road and climb along a lane through pine forest.

9 ☐ Left at the first convenient and signposted path to the Piburger See.

10 ☐ Follow the lake shore either left or right to its outlet stream.

Two lakeside restaurants offer refreshment at the end of the walk. There is bathing in this lake, but be prepared to pay for the facility.

11 ☐ Turn right along the access road and follow it downhill, out of the forest and back across the river into Oetz.

B • AROUND THE
FALTEGARTENKÖGELE

7¹/₂ miles (12km). 4 hours. Moderate. 1,844ft (562m) climb.

The Faltegartenkögele — 7,171ft (2,185m) marks the westerly limits of the Stubai Alps, a range of mountains east and north of the Ötztal Alps. This is not a hard climb, the route follows a series of cleverly made paths, all using the easiest ground to reach their objective.

The high-level section of the walk skirts the upper limits of the pine-clad southern slopes above the Inn valley.

Starting at the Ochsengarten restaurant bus stop on the mountain road from Oetz to Sellrain, the walk first climbs to a broad pine-clad col and then down to the far side of the Faltegartenkögele ridge. Leaving the tree line for a while, the path next climbs to a vantage point marked by a cross on the summit of Bärlehnkreuz — 6,905ft (2,104m). Starting the descent, at first the path crosses a rocky slope, but soon joins a forest track. This is followed all the way to Silz in the Inn valley where the buses run frequently towards Oetz. Check the timetable beforehand at the tourist information office in Oetz.

The Route

1 ☐   Take the Sellrain post bus as far as the Ochsengarten restaurant in the upper Nedertal valley.

2 ☐   Follow the Haiming high-level road away from the restaurant and over a broad pine-clad col. Walk by forest road as far as Kohlplatz.

3 ☐   Turn right along a gravel surfaced forest track.

4 ☐   Bear right at a fork beyond some marshy ground.

5 ☐   Turn right on a woodland path and climb steeply beneath the shoulder of Faltegartenkögele.

6 ☐   Leave the upper edge of the pine forest and climb the rocky hillside to the summit cross on top of Bärlehnkreuz.

The west facing hillside is a good spot for yellow and white anemones, blue gentians and red alpenrose.

7 ☐   Turn left, downhill by a rough path. Take care on loose rock

above the tree line and slippery surfaces within the forest.

8 ☐   Join a forest access track at a water metering station.

There is an underground pipeline at this point carrying water from a series of reservoirs on the far side of the mountain range, to a power station near Stams in the Inn valley.

9 ☐   Walk downhill by the easy track, mostly under the shade of massive pine trees. Ignore side tracks.

10 ☐   At a 'T' junction, go right, downhill to a second junction and turn left.

11 ☐   Follow the track to the left, then right above Silz and enter the village close by its swimming pool.

There is an attractive waterfall on the edge of meadowland above the swimming pool.

12 ☐   Spare time to explore Silz before catching the bus back to Oetz.

Oetz

C • THE WETTERSEE

8 miles (13km). 5–6 hours. Moderate/Strenuous.
5,097ft (1,553m) climb.

The reward for this stiff climb is an alpine lake set in a high hollow amongst the dramatic twin eastern arms of the Wildgrat mountain — 9,761ft (2,974m). An alpine hut completes the picture of an idyllic mountain scene further enhanced by masses of tiny cushion plants and the startling blue of spring gentians in the foreground.

Starting from Habichen just along the road from Oetz, the way is unrelentingly uphill almost to within sight of the lake. Fortunately the final stage of this most exciting section of the walk is along a reasonably level path, beneath the Kreuzjoch ridge. The lake comes as a pleasant reward for the effort and the welcome sight of the Erlanger hut will give promise of relief to thirsts generated by the climb. For the return journey the route is downhill, but again is steep and not to be considered lightly. At first a rocky path leads away from the hut to join its access track by the side of the Leiersbach stream. Wandering downhill in a series of wide zigzags, the track reaches the Ötztal road at Neudorf near Umhausen, where the bus can be used for the last few miles back to base.

The Route

1 ☐ The walk begins in Habichen, the next village along the Ötztal from Oetz. Turn right into a side road a little way beyond the road bridge.

2 ☐ Beyond a couple of farm buildings, turn left across a rough stony field and over a small stream.

3 ☐ Bear right, uphill through the boulder-filled forest.

4 ☐ Drop down to, and go through the hamlet of Tumpen.

5 ☐ Go past the church and fork right at the end of the street.

6 ☐ Start to climb through the forest, passing wayside crosses and tiny shrines along the way.

7 ☐ At the foot of a series of crags, turn right at a footpath junction and climb through the forest, again passing crosses and shrines.

8 ☐   Pause at the Gensteinalm hut before continuing uphill towards the furthest limits of the pine forest.

9 ☐   Turn right at a path junction and climb beneath the eastern shoulder of the Kreuzjoch.

The summit of Kreuzjoch — 8,783ft (2,676m) is marked by a prominent cross, just visible from the lower path.

10 ☐   Go round a steep rocky spur and out on a more level path. Follow it across the face of the mountain.

The south facing slope below the Kreuzjoch is a good area to hunt for alpine flowers. Many of them are quite rare. Photograph them by all means, but please never pick them, as it only lessens their chances of producing seed.

11 ☐   At a path junction, start to walk downhill over the steep scree-filled hillside towards the Wettersee and the Erlanger hut — 8,369ft (2,550m).

The lake marks the highest point of the walk. Enjoy the scene but remember that the downhill walk will still be tiring.

12 ☐   Go steeply downhill to the left of the hut, roughly parallel to its service cable, into the Leiersbach valley.

Cheeky whistles will indicate the presence of marmots, and chamois may also be seen crossing nearby mountain sides.

13 ☐   Join the access track and follow it steeply downhill into the forest.

14 ☐   Keep ahead at a track junction at point 1377.

15 ☐   Cross the river and walk uphill through the village of Neudorf and then go as far as Umhausen where the bus stop is in the centre of the village.

D • THE INN VALLEY

8 miles (13km). 3 hours. Easy.

This is a lazy day walk, or perhaps it can be used on a rainy day, which may happen in the Austrian Alps — even in summer!

The way is along the west bank of the lower reaches of the Ötztal river to its junction with the Inn. Then over the busy main road by the side of the River Inn and through the quiet village of Mairhof. An easy pine-covered hillside then leads back into the Ötztal from where the route goes back again through the pleasant village of Sautens to reach Oetz.

The Route

1 ☐   Follow the side road downstream and away from Oetz as far as the village of Sautens.

2 ☐   Go through the village and turn right past the church and then left before reaching the swimming pool.

3 ☐   Walk through meadowland and past two interesting and highly decorated wayside chapels.

4 ☐   Turn right at a track junction by a house called Rammelstein. Skirt the edge of a pine wood.

5 ☐   Fork right and enter the pine wood. Follow the left bank of the river as far as the main road.

6 ☐   Go under the road and again follow the Ötztaler Ache until it joins the Inn. Go under the railway line.

A new section (1986) of the Inn valley Autobahn *(the A12) has been carefully built high above the river across the opposite mountainside.*

7 ☐   Turn left and follow the River Inn upstream.

8 ☐   Join a small trackside road and go back under the railway line.

The power of the Inn can be appreciated at close quarters along the walk. Its colour is from sediment brought down from glaciers near its birth in Switzerland, or from tributaries further downstream from the source.

9 ☐ Cross the main road with care, and go through the village of Mairhof as far as the church.

10 ☐ Cross the square in front of the church.

11 ☐ Climb away from the village centre and into gently sloping meadowland.

12 ☐ Take each left fork towards the outer village limits and enter the pine forest.

13 ☐ Continue to climb, then bear left around the hillside along a quiet forest road.

14 ☐ At a junction of four forest roads, turn left downhill along a road marked by a series of calvary shrines.

15 ☐ Fork right past the Kreuzkapelle sports ground and walk down the road into Sautens. The walk then retraces its outward course.

16 ☐ Follow the road down to the river and turn right, upstream.

17 ☐ Join the Piburg road and turn left across the bridge into Oetz.

A traditional procession in the Ötztal

E • HOCHBRUNNACHKOGEL

9miles (14km). 5/6 hours. Strenuous. 2,560ft (780m) climb.

Here is a day out amongst the peaks! The route should be safe for anyone used to reasonably tough hill walking; the only proviso being that if there is any late snow on either side of the Niederreich Scharte col, then in prudence one should not be afraid to turn back. Fortunately the road from which the walk begins is served by a post bus route, so any retreat would only be as far as the road.

Climbing from the roadside, the path follows a narrow valley with high limestone peaks rising on either hand. Beyond the headwaters of the valley stream, the path climbs rapidly over the scree-covered lower slopes of the Hochbrunnach Kogel — 9,478ft (2,888m) and its taller neighbour the Grosser Wechnerkogel — 9,698ft (2,955m). A tiny lake, more a pool, adds interest to the climb. At the summit of the Niederreich Scharte — 8,953ft (2,728m), the highest point of the walk, an easier path gradually loses height before crossing the tree line and following a steep zigzag route down through pine forest to Oetz.

The Route

1 ☐   Take the post bus along Sellrain high-level road as far as the Dortmunder hut — 6,393ft (1,948m) and the start of the long climb.

2 ☐   Follow the Längental valley path round the east shore of the reservoir and beyond the Unter Längentalm *Gasthof*.

The Speicher Längental reservoir is part of a complex system of water collection to serve a power station at Silz in the Inn valley.

3 ☐   Go past the inflow pipeline and follow the path to the left of the Längental stream. Walk through scrubby pine woods which eventually give way to juniper bushes higher up the valley.

4 ☐   Cross the stream and climb the scree slope ahead.

5 ☐   Pause at the tiny pool below the Roter Kogel, and perhaps bathe your tired feet in its cool waters.

6 ☐   Swing round the lower slopes of the towering peaks of Hochbrunnachkogel and the Grosser Wechnerkogel.

7 ☐   Pause at the Niederreich Scharte col — 8,953ft (2,728m).

A spring on the col will offer a cool drink, if it is running!

8 ☐ Turn right and cross the rocky hillside towards the side ridge of the Hochbrunnachkogel.

9 ☐ At point 2611 the minor summit called Tauser, go steeply downhill through outcropping crags and then down scree slopes.

10 ☐ From point 2423 — Achplatte, swing right across a series of crags to the ruined Alte Bielefelder hut.

11 ☐ Turn sharp left at the hut, at a junction of five paths.

12 ☐ Go downhill into the forest to the Acherbergalm hut.

13 ☐ Turn left, downhill through forest.

14 ☐ Take the second, signposted path on the right and zigzag towards the Ederbach valley.

15 ☐ Turn right at a path junction and follow this route back to Oetz entering the village by going under the chairlift to join the Sellrain road.

16 ☐ Turn right along the road and then left through the upper outskirts of Oetz to reach the village centre.

F • THE VENET RIDGE WALK

7$\frac{1}{2}$ miles (12km). 4 hours. Moderate.

From Zams to the west, near Landeck in the Inn valley, the Venetbahn cable car climbs the west end of the Venet ridge. From here it is an easy scramble along the crest of the ridge and across a series of summits which rise above the general level of the ridge. The downhill path joins a forest track conveniently served by a pleasant *Gasthof*, well situated to cope with thirsts and hunger generated by this pleasant scramble.

The track leads downhill, beneath the shade of huge pines, to reach the valley road at Imsterberg.

Motorists are recommended to leave their cars at Zams or Imsterberg and catch the post bus in either direction. Non-motorists will need to plan this part of the walk more carefully. Details of the bus service are, of course, available from the Oetz tourist office.

The Route

1 ☐ Use the Venetbahn cable car from Zams to reach the summit

of Krahberg and the Panoramarestaurant at 7,247ft (2,208m).

2 ☐ Follow the footpath at first beneath a couple of ski-lifts, then over a small rise.

3 ☐ Walk ahead at a path and track junction, keeping to the summit of the ridge.

The ridge is an excellent place for alpine flowers and also as a viewpoint for the surrounding mountain ranges on either side of the Inn valley.

4 ☐ Ignoring side paths, continue forwards over the summit of the Glanderspitz — 8,244ft (2,512m) which is marked by a prominent cross.

5 ☐ Cross the intervening rocky slope and descend slightly to the Wannejöchl col – - 8,195ft (2,497m).

6 ☐ Go forwards over the rock and grass-covered ridge to Kreuzjoch — 7,962ft (2,426m).

7 ☐ Fork right at point 2381 and go downhill along the grassy side spur to enter the pine forest.

8 ☐ Stop at the Venetalphütte, or the Gamsteinhütte a little further downhill.

9 ☐ Turn left at the Gamsteinhütte and follow the forest road downhill.

10 ☐ Bear right at the first junction, then left at point 1787.

11 ☐ Swing round to the right, still on the forest road, then by a side path past the group of farms which fill the clearing at Eggwiese.

12 ☐ Above the ravine of the upper Kogelbach, join a track and follow it to the left and downhill back into the forest.

13 ☐ At a signpost, turn right on to a path and follow it into Imsterberg.

There is a curious and awe-inspiring ritual held every Christmas at Landeck, the major town in this part of the valley. At dusk huge bonfires are lit on the surrounding crags — such as the Venet ridge — and disks of pinewood dipped in tar oil are set alight and rolled down the hillsides. The ceremony is completed by a torchlight procession of young men racing down the mountains on skis at breakneck speed, all the time uttering blood-curdling yells.

G • THE GLEIRSCH, ZWISELBACH AND HORLACH VALLEYS

12$^1/_2$ miles (20km). 7 hours. Moderate/Strenuous.
4,060ft (1,237m) climb.

The technical difficulties involved in this walk are not great, but it is a long route and there is a lot of uphill walking. The rewards on the other hand, far exceed the effort needed to reach the ever changing viewpoints, or remote valleys.

It is the valleys which are perhaps the most interesting features of this walk. All three are remote, but each has its own individual characteristics. Only the Horlachtal is settled to any appreciable extent. Farms in this valley are used during the summer months by farmers who bring their flocks of sheep and a few cattle from the main farms in the lower Ötztal. This system, known by the curious term 'transhumance' has been used since primitive man first settled the district. Long winters prevent permanent habitation, but once the snows have gone, the land is covered with lush alpine grasses. At this time animals can benefit from the long days of warm sunshine.

A valley access track leads along the lower Gleirschtal from St Sigmund-in-Sellrain — 4,966ft (1,513m), the latter reached by post bus. Climbing out of the valley past the Pforzheimer hut, the path crosses the Gleirschjoch Pass — 9,026ft (2,750m), a climb of over 4,000ft (1,220m) from the start of the walk. From here it is downhill into Zwiselbachtal and then more easily along the Horlachbachtal and its summer farms. A side track is taken next across the forested hillside before dropping down to Umhausen and the main valley.

The Route

1 ☐ Take the post bus to St Sigmund-in-Sellrain.

2 ☐ Follow the valley track, past the Hubertus Hotel and gently along the forested valley. The Gleirschalm hut offers an early coffee stop.

3 ☐ Leave the main forest and pass dwindling clumps of stunted pines.

The old farm at Vorder Gleirschalm is a relic of the old farming traditions of this valley.

4 □   At the foot of a service cable, fork right, steeply zigzagging up the scree-covered slope to the Pforzheimer hut.

5 □   Climb from the hut to the Gleirschjoch Pass.

6 □   Go down the rocky hillside, following a side stream into the valley, the Zwiselbachtal, to reach the Gubener hut.

7 □   Turn left from the hut and go down the track alongside the Horlbach river.

The old farm buildings in this valley are built in traditional style to weather the long and heavy winter snows.

8 □   Below the Berghof hut, enter forest and fork right along a side track.

9 □   Go through Bichl and slightly uphill across the rocky hillside.

10 □   Fork left, downhill by footpath, to meet a forest track.

11 □   Turn left along the track and follow it into Umhausen.

12 □   Catch the bus back to Oetz, unless your energies allow an extra road walk at the end of a long and tiring day.

H • AMBERG TO STAMS

9 miles (14km). 3–4 hours. Easy.

Most of the walks in this section have been fairly strenuous, so this final walk has been included as a gentle stroll at the end of what has probably been a fairly tough holiday. The series of forest tracks and paths which the route follows are all well graded and in fact are mostly downhill!

After an initial pull, away from the Sellrain road, the track crosses a low col to the east of the little hillock of Amberg. From this point the walk is downhill and across the wide forested hillside of the Stubai Massif. A diversion above Silz will take in an attractive waterfall, then the way is easy down to Stams.

The Route

1 □   Take the Sellrain post bus to the Amberg turning, a little way

below the steep hairpins near Balbach. Ask the bus driver to make an unscheduled stop at Amberg or walk back if he/she is unwilling.

2 ☐ Turn left from the road and follow the track uphill across the slope of the Ochsengarten forest.

3 ☐ Reach the low col at Amberg.

To the right of the track and partly hidden in the forest is a small lake, the Amberger See, which makes an interesting diversion.

4 ☐ Bear right, away from the col, downhill towards the Haiming road.

5 ☐ Turn left downhill along the road.

6 ☐ After about 1$^1/_2$ miles (2km) turn right on a small side track towards a group of hillside farms.

7 ☐ Take the left fork and walk as far as the Alpenblick *Gasthof.*

8 ☐ Left between the Alpenblick and a shrine, steeply downhill across the meadow and through forest. Follow a line of crosses.

9 ☐ Join a narrow track, turn right and walk across the hillside.

A signpost marks a diversion to a small waterfall. Return to the track and turn left along it.

10 ☐ Climb to a track junction and cross the stream, the Stadliger Bach. Keep ahead on the track which gradually narrows into a footpath.

11 ☐ Join a forest road on a sharp bend. Turn left, downhill and follow it into the village of Stams.

Stams has a number of shops and small cafés, but its most interesting feature is the thirteenth-century Cistercian abbey, rebuilt in the eighteenth century. An architectural gem, the abbey church is the largest baroque-style church in the Tyrol. Inside the decor is by such masters as Feuchtmayer and Vischer.

4 LEUTASCH

Map

Kompass Wanderkarte (1:25,000 scale) Sheet 026; Seefeld in Tirol.
Or Freytag and Berndt Wanderkarte (1:50,000 scale) Sheet WK 322
— Wetterstein-Karwendel; Seefeld-Leutasch; Garmisch Parten-
kirchen.

How to Get There

Road

1 • Via the German *Autobahn* system to Munich, then south by the E6
to Garmisch-Partenkirchen. Alternatively leave the *Autobahn* at
Augsburg, then south via Landsberg and Peiting to Garmisch-Partenkirchen. South-east to Mittenwald and then the minor road south-
west, over the border into the Leutasch valley.

2 • South by the European motorway system to Basel. East through
Switzerland via Zurich and the south shore of Lake Constance
(Bodensee) to the Austrian border. East along the E17 via the Arlberg
(pass or tunnel) to Telfs. North-east by minor road to Leutasch.

Rail

1 • Trans-European service to Innsbruck and local post bus to
Leutasch via Seefeld.

2 • Via Munich, then south to Seefeld followed by the post bus.

Air

1 • Regular flights from London (Gatwick), to Innsbruck airport
followed by train or post bus via Seefeld.

2 • International flights to Munich followed by train to Seefeld and post
bus to Leutasch.

The Area

Leutasch is situated to the north-west of the Seefeld basin, far less
well known than its touristy and more expensive big sister Seefeld,
where coach loads of tourists 'doing' the Alps, or perhaps on their way
to the Italian Lake District, spend a night.

It is a great pity that they and more independent tourists, do not
spend a little longer in the area, for here in the north-west of the high
hollow made famous by the Winter Olympics, is an area of delectable

mountain walking. The Seefeld basin is sheltered by the massive wall of the Wetterstein range to the north and also separated from busy Seefeld town to the south, by the wooded slopes of Hochmoos hill. The walking is ideal for those who want to enjoy the scenery and forests with the minimum of effort. The Wetterstein are limestone mountains which are almost the mirror image of the Dolomites in the south. They started as calcareous sludge in the bottom of a tropical sea millions of years ago and together with the rest of the Alps were thrust high by earth movements and later worn into their present shape by glacial action. Both ranges mark the north–south extremities of the Alps, beyond which are vast plains, the Venetian plain in the case of the Dolomites, and the Bavarian plain which stretches away to Munich and beyond on the northern side of the Wetterstein range.

Leutasch is claimed to be the longest village in Austria. Strictly speaking it is a series of inter-dependent villages and hamlets filling the sunny bowl of the lower Leutascher Ache. Far quieter than neighbouring Seefeld, it is protected to the north by the bare limestone ridges of the Wetterstein. Their forested lower slopes offer miles of easy walking, while the more ambitious mountain walker can easily reach accessible local peaks and ridges without having to resort to alpine climbing techniques.

The valley is an ideal base to use as a jumping off point for places such as Innsbruck and the whole of the central Inn valley. Mayrhofen and the famous Zillertal railway are not too far away, neither are the Stubai and Ötztal valleys.

Bavaria is to the north and such famous places as Oberammergau and its links with the Passion Play are only an hour's drive away. King Lüdwig of Bavaria's fairy-tale castles of Neuschwanstein and Linderhof are within easy reach. Likewise the Zugspitze, Germany's highest mountain can be climbed quite easily by any of its cable cars or the funicular railway. A trip into Italy is an easy proposition, but perhaps the most enjoyable and most accessible excursion is made on foot to Mittenwald. This German border town is filled with houses attractively decorated with wall paintings, but its most interesting feature is the museum devoted to violin-making, a traditional industry which is continued in the town to this day.

The Leutasch valley provides all the usual facilities one expects from an alpine resort. Farmhouse restaurants and mountain huts offer refreshment throughout the area. The upper valley has only two chairlifts, but the Seefelder Spitze and Reither Spitze above Seefeld are well served by a funicular railway and two cable cars (with an extra one planned). Shops in the Leutasch valley cater mainly for local needs, leaving the more sophisticated shopping to Seefeld. Post buses, local taxis and coaches can be relied upon for transport.

Useful Information

Tourist Office
Fremdenverkehrsverband Leutasch
A-6105 Leutasch-Tirol
☎ (05214) 6207
Accommodation ranges from five-star international hotels in nearby Seefeld to homely *Gasthöfe*, rented apartments and one camp site.

Cable Cars and Chairlifts
Leutasch
Mundelift Chairlift from Moos (upper valley) to the Mundeblick hut beneath the eastern slopes of the Hohe Munde.
Kreitlift Chairlift from Unterweidach to the Katsenkopf Bergrestaurant. Used also for access to the top of the Rolba Run, an exciting summer toboggan run of $^3/_4$ mile (1.2km).
Seefeld
Funicular railway from Seefeld to the Rosshütte. Cable car from the Rosshütte giving access to the Seefelder Joch and Seefelder Spitze.
Härmelekopfbahn From the Rosshütte. Can be used on the final leg of the high ridge walk over the Seefelder Spitze and the Reither Spitze to cut out the long walk back to Seefeld.

Swimming
Pools in the Leutascher Ache are ideal for impromptu bathing. The Alpenbad in Weidach is more formal. Remember to obtain a *Gästkarte* if staying in the valley, this will give a reduction on the entry fee and also cover other amenities in the area.

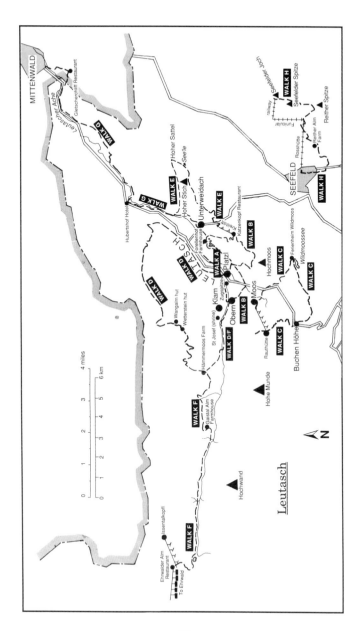

MITTENWALD

Gletscherschliff Restaurant

Leutascher Ache

WALK G

WALK E
Hoher Sattel
See'le

Hubertshof Höhe

WALK G
WALK E
Hoher Stich
Unterweidach

WALK E
Katzenkopf Restaurant

WALK C
Forellenhof
Farmhouse

WALK A
Platzl

WALK B
Hochmoos

Ferienheim Wildmoos
Wildmoossee

WALK C

Hoher Sattel

WALK E

Hochmoos

WALK C

Klainbach

Buchen Höhe

Reither Alm
Farm

Reither Spitze

Rosshütte

SEEFELD

WALK H

railway   Seefelder Joch

WALK H
Seefelder Spitze

Funicular

WALK D

Wangalm hut

Wetterstein hut

St Josef (shrine)

WALK D/F

Klam
Zugspitze

Obern

WALK B

Moos

Rauchhütte

WALK C

Hämmermoos Farm

Hohe Munde

4 miles
6 km
0 1 2 3 4 5
0 1 2 3

N

WALK F
Gaistal Alm
Farmhouse

Hochwand

Leutasch

Ehrwalder Alm
Restaurant

Issentalkopfl

WALK F

To Ehrwald

73

A • THE LEUTASCH VALLEY

4 miles (6.4km). 2 hours. Easy.

There are usually one or two mundane tasks necessary on the first day of a holiday. Visits to the bank, the local shops, and where to find the Tourist Information Office. This walk is designed to include these facilities, and starts (and finishes) at the local Spar supermarket, a tiny general store selling practically everything likely to be required during the holiday.

About half way round the walk there is a bank, where the extended opening hours are convenient for holiday makers, however, like most offices in Austria, the bank will close for a couple of hours at lunchtime.

Although the walk can be joined more or less anywhere along its route, it starts in Platzl, the central hamlet of the Leutasch group of villages. Quickly leaving the meadows in the valley bottom, it climbs into the Schlagwald forest, cloaking the slopes of Katzenkopf to the south. Turning east on woodland tracks, the route passes first the trout ponds, then the lake of Weidachsee. A little road walking follows, through Oberweidach where a riverside track leads to Kirchplatzl, the main village in the valley. Not only is the police station here, but there is a bank, post office and information centre, all within the same complex. An easy riverside walk leads back to Platzl.

The Route

1 ☐ Almost opposite the Spar supermarket in Platzl, a lane leads south-east across meadowland and into the forest. Follow it as far as a junction of four tracks and paths.

2 ☐ Cross the forest track and climb gently beneath the tall pines.

3 ☐ Fork left after 275yd (250m) and walk over the forested rise for another 500yd (460m) and fork right at a junction with a wide track.

4 ☐ Turn right along the improving track and walk past Weidachsee.

Trout bred in the upper and lower pools are usually on sale at the Forellenhof farmhouse just beyond the main lake. Angling is permitted in the lake, but check at the Forellenhof for permits.

5 ☐ Turn left by the lower trout pools and walk along the lane as far as the road. Turn left and walk to the river. Do not cross the bridge.

74

Walking near Leutasch

6 ☐ Turn left upstream on the river bank. Turn right at the next bridge if requiring the bank or post office.

The bank, post office and information centre are in the building on the left, on the main road, at the end of the track beyond the river.

The clear inviting water of the Leutascher Ache drain the limestone slopes of the lower Wetterstein mountains. In summer the river is a mere trickle of its rampaging late spring self, when it carries water from melting snow.

7 ☐ Return to the river. Cross over and turn right upstream beneath the shade of riverside trees and bushes. Follow this track, parallel to the road.

8 ☐ Look out for a signpost to the Zugspitze Hotel prior to the second road bridge. Turn left along the road. The Spar shop is about 200yd (180m) on the right.

B • HOCHMOOS

8 miles (12.8km). 5–6 hours. Moderate.
689ft (210m) ascent.

The forested slopes of Hochmoos seem to dominate the Leutasch valley, despite their lack of height. An impudent little hill compared with the brooding giants of the Wetterstein range to the north and the steep slopes of Hohe Munde to the west. It is perhaps the contrast of Katzenkopf's forest against the bare limestone ridges and summits of the high peaks, which draws the eye southwards to its dark brooding pines. This walk is ideal for a hot day and even though the initial climb is fairly steep, it does not offer any real hardship.

The route is easy to follow apart from one or two tricky junctions. Waymarking is mainly blue paint splashes on trees or rocks and much of the way is signposted. Starting at Obern to the west of the Leutasch valley, and after an initial easy ascent, the path climbs steeply to the crest of the Schlagwald ridge. Turning east, the way is then to the Katzenkopf restaurant and the descent over Rappenlocher, a crag with an excellent view of the valley.

The Route

1 ☐   Start by the wayside chapel in Obern and walk south-south-east along a farm lane towards the forest edge at Ostbachbrücke.

2 ☐   Walk through the forest as far as the road at Ostbachbrücke. Turn right, then left along a forest track as far as a crossing of tracks by the side of a small gravel pit. The turning is unmarked and the track crossing is used purely as a reference point.

3 ☐   Walk back along the track for about 160yd (150m) and turn left on a forest path.

4 ☐   Climb steadily uphill beneath the mature pine trees, following the zigzagging path and also blue waymark signs.

There is a good view on the way up, of the Hohe Munde –– 8,727ft (2,659m), across the valley.

5 ☐   Bear left (to the east-south-east), still climbing until a forest driveway is reached. Turn left then right just before a sharp bend in the roadway.

6 ☐   Climb the narrow path towards a small clearing.

7 □   Turn left at an indistinct footpath junction and walk on towards a viewpoint and a group of seats and the end of the climb.

The Hohen Aussichtspunkt (high viewpoint) will make an excellent rest place. Admire the view of the Wetterstein range across the valley.

8 □   Walk on downhill away from the viewpoint, following blue waymarks.

9 □   Turn left on the forest track towards the Katzenkopf restaurant and chairlift.

Adventurous members of the party may wish to use the 'all-year-round' toboggan run to reach the lower valley. Otherwise follow the next set of directions.

10 □   Turn left away from the restaurant to follow the signposted path towards the crag of Rappenlöcher.

Rappenlöcher has an attractive view of the lower valley and the Wetterstein peaks.

11 □   Walk down into Unterweidach village and turn left.

12 □   Follow the road as far as the river and turn left.

13 □   Follow the riverside path, upstream as far as the road into Obern and turn left.

Leutasch valley and the Hohe Munde

C • BUCHEN HÖHE

6$^{1}/_{2}$ miles (10.4km). 4 hours. Easy/Moderate.
1,431ft (436m) descent.

Variation is the keyword of this walk. The views vary between the majesty of the Wetterstein range including Zugspitze, with the deep trough of the Inn valley to the south; mountain scenery gives way gradually to forest and there are even the tailored fairways of a golf course on this walk. It is not particularly long or difficult, but it is certainly one of constant change and a walk to spend all day over. On no account should the many and varied viewpoints be neglected.

The walk starts quite high on the shoulder of the Hohe Munde peak; height gained in comfort by the Mundelift chairlift. Downhill walking through forest leads on to Buchen and the interesting farm museum. Gentle forest walking across and above the Seefeld golf course preludes an easy climb along the Schlagsteig path back to Moos and the Mundelift car park.

The Route

1 □   Either walk, drive or take the bus, to the head of the Leutasch valley as far as Moos and take the Mundelift chairlift to its top station.

2 □   From the Rauthütte near the top of the lift, follow the signpost to the right to the Zugspitze viewpoint.

The Zugspitze, Germany's highest mountain, is the snow clad peak at the western end of the Wetterstein range.

Hang gliding is a popular sport on these lower slopes of the Hohe Munde mountain; the take-off point is close by the viewpoint.

3 □   Return to the Rauthütte and follow the signposted path downhill to the left of the top station. Follow it in the direction of Buchen Hohe and Katzenloch.

4 □   Follow the steep rocky path down the pine-clad slope and past occasional beech trees. Keep well to the left of the Glatte Wand gorge if in any doubt at junctions with 'unofficial' side paths.

Pause to admire the views of the Inn valley far below. The first town to come into view is Telfs and later Zirl, marked by its complex Autobahn *junction with the road from Mittenwald and Seefeld.*

5 ☐ At the path junction in Katzenloch, turn right, downhill on a broad path as far as the road.

6 ☐ Follow the signposted track, which runs parallel with the road, to Buchen Höhe and the farm museum.

The farm museum, which is free to enter, is a small, but well composed collection of local farming and farmhouse equipment from bygone days.

7 ☐ Follow the grassy track across a meadow, walking slightly uphill, beyond the museum and its restaurant. Go under a ski-tow cable and enter the forest.

8 ☐ Follow signs pointing to Wildmoos.

9 ☐ Drop down to the golf course and carefully follow the path between its fairways, continuing as directed by the Wildmoos signs.

10 ☐ Walk along a rough lane, through a gate and past the Ferien-heim Wildmoos.

(A Ferienheim *is a holiday home for groups and families and is a common feature in Austria and Germany.)*

The Wildmoossee on the right of the Ferienheim *is likely to be dried up during anything but torrential rain.*

11 ☐ Turn left around the *Ferienheim*, uphill on a forest track, the Schlagsteig.

12 ☐ Look out for blue waymarks indicating the true route where the track disintegrates into a complex of forest tracks and footpaths. Walk ahead, uphill through the trees.

13 ☐ Go steeply downhill and turn right on joining a gravel track.

14 ☐ Leave the track at a signpost to Moos. Follow the path through trees and out into open meadowland and the valley road. The Mundelift car park is beyond and to the left.

D • MOOSALM AND THE PUITTAL

12 miles (19.3km). 7–8 hours. Strenuous.
2,901ft (884m) ascent.

The long line of the Wetterstein range marking the border between Austria and Germany, will surely attract the eye of all mountain lovers. Its sheer limestone walls and serrated ridges dominate the northern skyline of the Leutasch valley. On this walk, paths reach as high beneath the crags as it is possible to go, without involving walkers in rock climbing. At no time during the walk does the route stray from paths which are within the capabilities of the average hillwalker. The walk, however, is long and arduous, covering a wild upland area between the main Wetterstein range and their satellites, the Gehren-spitze — 7,768ft (2,367m).

The route starts along the Gaistal to the west of Leutasch, and climbs its northern hillside by the easiest route. This goes by way of the Hämmermoosalm farm to avoid a steep and rough track up the Klammbach valley, to the Wetterstein and Wangalm huts, before climbing the Scharnitz Joch and descending to the main Leutasch valley along the Puittal, which is a good example of a glacial 'hanging' valley. A long walk, but one which is highly recommended.

The Route

1 ☐ Start from Obern and walk along the road to the river. Turn left on the valley road for about ¹/₄ mile (402m) and left again over a footbridge.

2 ☐ Turn right along the riverside path, following it as far as a second footbridge. Go across the bridge then left along the road and through a narrow rocky gorge.

3 ☐ Cross the river again by a third footbridge and continue to walk upstream.

At the third footbridge, look back and up to the religious sculptures of the shrine to St Joseph high in the crag.

4 ☐ Cross the river for the last time. Turn left on the road for about 50yd (46m) and right on a woodland track signposted to Hämmermoos.

5 ☐ Leave the track and follow the waymarked path steeply uphill

through the forest and out on to rough hillside grazing.

6 □ Turn right along the access lane to Hämmermoosalm farm.

Hämmermoosalm farm makes an ideal early stopping place. Milk not used for cheese is sold by the glass and is delightfully cool on a hot day.

7 □ Continue along the track beyond the farm and up to the wooded hillside.

8 □ Bear right across the hillside on what becomes a waymarked (in red) footpath. Follow it to the Wetterstein hut — 5,635ft (1,717m).

The Wetterstein hut will probably be reached about lunchtime; its balcony is an ideal open-air dining area, where the views across the Leutasch basin take in the Hohe Munde and beyond to the Stubai Alps, across the deep trough of the Inn valley.

9 □ Drop down to the stream and climb past the Wangalm hut. Continue uphill along a grassy path.

10 □ Enter the rocky zone beneath the screes of the Wetterstein range and bear right around the upper combe.

A boulder in the upper combe by the side of the path is a memorial stone to local climbers and others who have died in these and other mountains further afield.

11 □ Cross the Scharnitz Joch — 6,728ft (2,050m).

Pause to admire the magnificent view from the top of the pass and also the southern crags of the south wall of the Wetterstein mountains.

12 □ Walk downhill into the Puittal on a rough path. Take care to keep to the route when crossing areas of stones washed down by spring floods and avalanches.

13 □ Enter the lower alpine zone of scrub pine and mountain grazing for local cattle.

Flowers abound in this area, especially alpenrose.

14 □ Walk down the valley as far as a boundary fence. Go through a small gate and begin to zigzag steeply downhill into pine forest.

The fence marks the lip of a hanging valley formed by the more powerful and deeper glacier which filled the main valley in the Ice Age. It scoured the valley sides leaving Puittal relatively unchanged, its shape formed by its own smaller glacier.

15 ☐   At the bottom of the zigzags, turn right and cross a plank bridge. Walk through the last of the pines and out onto an open meadow.

16 ☐   Enter the village of Lehner and bear right along the signposted 'Sudprommenade' footpath. Follow it into Kirchplatzl.

Several Gasthöfe *and hotels are passed along the way and will no doubt be welcomed for the refreshments they offer.*

17 ☐   Walk to the river by any of the side roads. Cross over and turn right.

18 ☐   Follow the river upstream as far as the bridge near Obern. Turn right to reach the village.

E • SATTELTAL

$5^1/_2$ miles (9km). 4 hours. Moderate.
1,726ft (526m) ascent.

The Puittal walk was mostly in open country which can be exceptionally tiring in hot weather. If the weather is still fine, the shade of the Neuwald will come as a welcome relief. The climb is straightforward all the way to Hoher Sattel and then a fairly steep climb leads to some of the best and most natural woodland in the area. Wide ranging views open from time to time, one of them taking in Puittal. At the end of the walk, the Kreith chairlift might tempt the more adventurous into a ride to its top station, followed by a wild exhilarating run down the dry toboggan run — the Rolba. The run is a concrete structure of innumerable bends, all carefully banked so that they may be taken at maximum speed. The bobs have handbrakes enabling the rider to control the speed to his or her skill.

The Route

1 ☐   The walk starts from Unterweidach. Walk down the lane at the side of bank.

2 ☐   Do not turn left for the river, but carry on along the side road until the last houses are left behind.

3 ☐   Turn right on joining an uphill track by the side of the river bed.

4 ☐   Climb the stony forest track which is steep in places, beneath mature pine trees. Follow this all the way to the col at Hoher Sattel — 4,874ft (1,485m).

The col is about the only area of open ground encountered on the walk and makes an ideal picnic spot.

5 ☐   Turn right at the col following the direction of the wooden signpost.

6 ☐   Climb steeply beneath the trees following the path round the forested hillside spur.

7 ☐   Ignore side paths and start to descend on the narrow path.

Sheltered platforms on the top of tall narrow timber towers, seen at intervals along the walk, are used by hunters during the shooting season, to sit quietly and wait for deer to come into the sights of their rifles.

Most maps show a small pond called See'le, but this is now no more than a swamp with a couple of tiny pools, the breeding ground of mosquitos!

More views open up all the while, this time of the Seefeld basin and Katzenkopfe beyond Weidach.

8 ☐   The path merges with a forest track. Follow it downhill.

9 ☐   At the signposted junction ignore the direction to Unterweidach, but continue along the forest track.

10 ☐   At the next bend where there is a second signpost, bear right, still on the track and walk downhill to Kreith, the southern outskirts of Weidach.

11 ☐   Turn right at the road to reach the centre of Weidach and its shops and restaurants.

The Kreithlift is opposite the point where the forest track joins the road. If intending to finish this walk on an exciting toboggan ride, turn left, then right, to reach the bottom of the chairlift. A ride on the Rolba Run is highly recommended! According to the proprietors, the run is about $^3/_4$ mile long (1.2km) and descends 755ft (230m) through fifty bends.

F • GAISTAL

10 miles (16km). 4–5 hours. Easy.

Even though it is possible for a strong party to do this walk in both directions in a day, it is recommended that transport arrangements are made to Ehrwald for the start of the walk. The drive will be interesting enough, probably via the old road through Telfs, way above the Inn valley. The route is then via the Fernpass to Lermoos with Ehrwald to the east, across the wide Lermoos basin. A cable car ride takes much of the effort out of the climb to the col, which is the start of the descent to the Gaistal.

The walk is straightforward, following the valley track most of the way, but with variations to visit hospitable huts and farmhouses. The views are of mountains and torrents shrouded by forests.

The Route

1 ☐ Use the cable car from Ehrwald to reach the Ehrwalderalm restaurant.

2 ☐ Follow the side track away from the restaurant. Go under a chairlift and cross the junction of two rocky streambeds. Walk on past the Alpenglühn hut.

The snow-capped summit of the Zugspitze — 9,721ft (2,962m) peeps over the Wetterstein ridge to the north of the path.

3 ☐ At a hairpin bend by the side of a stream turn left and follow the true left bank of the stream. (The stream should then be on your right). The way is now mostly in forest.

4 ☐ Climb to a footpath junction marked by an alpine chapel.

Look across the Fern Pass towards the Lech mountains.

5 ☐ Pass a track junction marked by a wayside cross and begin to walk downhill into denser pine forest.

6 ☐ Cross three rocky streambeds and descend by any convenient path towards the valley track.

The southern wall of the Gaistal valley is dominated by the limestone peaks of Hochwand — 8,924ft (2,719m) and Hohe Munde— 8,737ft (2,662m), their lower slopes densely forested, but bare rock appears higher up. Areas of hillside free of forest have often been denuded by avalanches in past winters.

7 ☐　Turn left along the track, following it gradually downhill.

8 ☐　Turn left along the signposted access track up to the Gaistal Alm farmhouse where the ice cold milk is delicious.

9 ☐　Climb by track away from the farm for about $\frac{1}{3}$ mile (536m) and turn right, on an indistinct and unmarked path across almost park-like pasture. Do not worry if you do not strike the path immediately, the secret is to keep to the left of the upper edge of the forest. The path becomes apparent later on.

10 ☐　Drop into a narrow wooded gorge and cross the stream at a footbridge, then walk on along the wide track.

11 ☐　Turn left on a narrow path signposted to Hämmermoos Alm.

12 ☐　A faint and again unmarked grassy footpath leaves the access track about 100yd (91m) below the farm. Follow this downhill to the left and below the farm, across meadowland and through forest to the valley track.

14 ☐　Turn left along the track. Go right by the gate above the car park. Cross the river and follow a shady path, to the left downstream, crossing and recrossing the river by footbridges to avoid road walking.

15 ☐　The walk ends at the road bridge between Klamm and Obern.

The Leutasch river

G • BY THE LEUTASCHKLAMM TO MITTENWALD

11 miles (17.7km). 5 hours. Easy.

Walking in a mountainous region need not be at high altitude for the walker to enjoy the mountains. Here is such a walk; for most of the way it is relatively flat, following the course of the Leutasch river, the Leutascher Ache. It goes through the scattered hamlets of Leutasch and the lush riverside meadows, where it enters an area of forest. The path follows a crystal clear stream where the view has been described as more like the Canadian Rockies than the Austrian Tyrol, downstream to the Austro-German border. At this point the river plunges through a narrow gorge, the Leutaschklamm, the only break in the border ridge. Then the route climbs slightly, away from the ravine, before descending steeply towards the bottom end of the Leutaschklamm, where for a small fee you may walk into the heart of the gorge, on a wooden path projecting from the rocky wall. Such is the variation of scenery on this walk.

Leutaschklamm

The Route

1 ☐   The walk starts from Obern in the upper Leutasch basin, but could easily be joined at any convenient point along the valley. Walk down to the river bridge and turn right to follow the well defined path along the right bank of the Leutascher Ache downstream.

2 ☐   Cross valley roads four times, keeping the river and its bridges always on your left.

3 ☐   Beyond Unterweidach, cross over to the left bank of the river following it downstream to the next bridge. Turn right across the bridge then left, still downstream on the wide gravel path.

4 ☐   Still following the river, go past a camp site and as far as its access bridge then turn left. Walk along the road verge towards the Hubertshof Hotel (a good place for a coffee stop).

5 ☐   Follow the signposted path down to and over the river. Turn left and continue the downstream route along a clear path in and out of the lower forest.

6 ☐   Bear right as signposted (to Mittenwald) to follow a side stream of the main river. Note that this stream is not shown on most maps of the area.

The crystal waters of this side stream contrast with the milky texture of the main river. Speckled trout live in its clear depths and the view of the nearby peaks through the wild pine forest could easily be mistaken for Canada.

7 ☐   Join the road by the old mill restaurant. Walk on the left to face oncoming traffic, towards the customs post.

It is most unlikely that you will be stopped at the customs post, but passports should be carried just in case. The actual border is about $1^1/_2$ miles (2.4km) further on at the narrowest point of the gorge.

8 ☐   Where the road crosses a bridge above the customs post, turn right along a signposted (to Mittenwald) forest track. Climb steadily around the northern flank of Wildstkopf — 5,087ft (1,550m).

9 ☐   Cross the marked border into Germany and walk down to the Gletscherschliff restaurant.

The restaurant comes as a welcome break, but remember it is in Germany and you will probably need Deutschmarks!

10 ☐   Walk down the access track and join the track into Mittenwald. Turn left for the town centre.

The entrance to the Leutaschklamm is to the left at the lowest point of the path below the restaurant.

For the return journey to Leutasch there is a late afternoon bus, or the train could be used as far as Seefeld. Check times locally.

The Reither Spitze

View from the Seefelder Spitze

H • THE REITHER SPITZE

5 miles (8km). 6 hours. Strenuous.
1,014ft (309m) ascent, 4,014ft (1,223m) descent.

This is a popular yet relatively easy climb for mountaineers visiting Seefeld. It crosses the Seefelder Spitze ridge, then climbs across the Reither Kar, a huge limestone scree-filled combe, before approaching the Reither Spitze. The final climb is steep and not for those without a good head for heights, but it is straightforward except when it is raining. In rain, or just after, the route can be positively dangerous and so should never be tried in anything but fine dry weather. It should go without saying that boots **must** be worn on this mountain expedition.

The initial climb is by way of the Rosshütte funicular railway, followed by the Seefelder Jochbahn cable car. Anyone in your party not wishing to complete the high-level section of the route could take the Härmelekopf cable car to its top station from the Rosshütte and meet the climbing members of the party for the descent back to Seefeld.

The Route

1 ☐　The walk starts and finishes at Seefeld railway station. Walk along Andreas Hofer Strasse to the signposted lower station of the Rosshütte Standseilbahn (funicular). Take this to the top station followed by the cable car to the Seefelder Joch.

2 ☐　Turn right away from the top station and walk along the grassy ridge to the summit of the Seefelder Spitze — 7,286ft (2,220m).

Admire both the extensive views of the Tyrolean mountains and also the flowers closer to hand.

3 ☐　Walk on downhill beneath the upended strata of the Torl ridge. Climb down into the scree-filled combe of Reither Kar. Follow the well maintained path to the left.

4 ☐　Climb up to the obvious narrow col of Reither Joch — 7,151ft (2,179m).

5 ☐　Turn left and follow the red waymarks to the summit of Reither Spitze — 7,788ft (2,373m). Return by the same route.

6 ☐　Two rocky paths lead away from the col. Either will suffice, but the left and lower is the easiest. Walk down to the top station of the Härmelekopf cable car.

As the path is followed downhill it passes through four distinct zones; the highest is the alpine, where minute flowers find life amongst the bare rocks and scree. Next is low scrub, which gives way to alpine pasture, the lower zone is forest and this is followed all the way to Seefeld.

Tall structures with prominent orange markings, on either side of the Reither Kar combe, are to warn aircraft pilots of the nearby cable-ways.

7 ☐　Bear left away from the cable, downhill through scrub and alpine pasture into the upper reaches of mature larch and pine forest. The path zigzags and is indistinct in places. Take care to follow the red waymarks.

8 ☐　Walk through the forest as far as the Reither Alm farmhouse restaurant, an ideal stopping place.

9 ☐　Follow the rocky path which crosses the farm's access track, steeply downhill through the forest to the access road into the Ichthyolwerk plastics factory. Turn right and walk along it as far as the main road.

The name 'Ichthyolwerk' refers to the local shale oil industry which took place before and during World War II. A number of mines and factories once dotted the hillside, but the plastics factory is now the only reminder.

10 ☐　Cross the main road with great care and turn right along a footpath which eventually links with the Römer Weg into Seefeld. The station is to the left on rejoining Andreas Hofer Strasse.

5 MAYRHOFEN

Map
Kompass Wanderkarte (1:50,000 series) Sheet 37 ; Zillertaler Alpen

How to Get There

Road

1 • South-east by the European motorway system to Munich, then south via the Tegernsee (Germany) and Achensee (Austria) to Jenbach and Wiesing into the Zillertal.

2 • Via the Black Forest and the north shore of Lake Constance (Bodensee) to Bregenz. East via the Arlberg Pass, or tunnel, into the Inn valley; then via Innsbruck to Wiesing and the turn off to the south for the Zillertal.

Rail

Main line services either via the Arlberg Express or from Munich to Innsbruck — local services to Jenbach and branch line to Mayrhofen.

Air

Either to Munich or Salzburg, then rail via Innsbruck or Jenbach. Alternatively, several airlines operating STOL aircraft such as the BAe 146, are now flying direct to Innsbruck's Kranebitten airport.

The Area

The Zillertal, and in particular Mayrhofen, has become extremely popular over the last decade with holidaymakers who wish to enjoy a relaxed holiday in a mountain environment. Many will only visit the main valley, preferring to let their eyes, rather than their feet, wander over the mountain heights. This is a great pity for it is an area which calls for close exploration. There are literally miles of carefully graded hillside footpaths and several mountain summits all well within the capabilities of anyone sound in wind and limb.

Mayrhofen sits at the end of the flat-bottomed Zillertal and from there, four side valleys, or *grund* to give them their local dialect name, radiate like a broad fan. The first, to the east with its new road, is the Zillergrund, really a continuation of the main valley. The Zillergrund is separated from the Stillupgrund by the Ahornspitze, a mountain at the end of a long complex ridge, radiating north from the Austro-Italian border. The next two valleys running south from Mayrhofen in close proximity to each other, are the Stillupgrund and Zemmgrund. Finally, in the west is the Tuxertal, narrow in its lower reaches near Mayrhofen, but broadening into a flat-bottomed lush grazing area around Vorderlanersbach. Roads reach quite high in all four valleys and so a car or the local post bus service, can be used to reach the start of many interesting walks.

To the north of Mayrhofen, at Zell am Ziller, a road climbs in a series of twists and turns over the wooded Gerlos Pass and then down into the Pinzgau valley. (See the Neukirchen chapter for walks in this area).

Folk music is important to the people living in the Zillertal; local choirs perform throughout the season, often accompanied by harps or zithers. Zither playing is especially renowned in the area. The beautiful Christmas hymn *Silent Night, Holy Night*, has links with the Ziller region, and might have disappeared had it not been for the observance of a local organ repairer. As mice had ruined their organ bellows, the hymn was originally composed as an emergency measure, to be sung accompanied by zither by the village choir of Oberndorf near Salzburg. Afterwards the text and score were stuffed behind the organ pipes and forgotten. The Zillertal organ repairer found them years later and took them home. About that time (it was the early nineteenth century) the valley was famous for its glove making and it was customary for local choirs and musicians to perform at trade fairs. Seeking a new approach, the Zillertal choir decided to sing the piece at the Leipzig Trade Fair; *Silent Night, Holy Night* , was an immediate success.

There are many alternatives to hill walking, ranging from *Tiroler Abend* which is evening entertainment with a local flavour; to cycle hire, horse-drawn carriage rides, hang gliding instruction, bowling, golf, squash, outdoor chess, fishing, or even summer skiing above Hintertux at the top end of the Tuxertal. Rail enthusiasts will enjoy a ride on the tiny steam train, the famous narrow gauge Zillertalbahn, which plies up and down the valley.

Useful Information

Local Tourist Office
Fremdenverkehrsverband   Mayrhofen
A-6290 Mayrhofen
☎ (05285) 2305 or 2635

Alpine meadows near Mayrhofen

Accommodation
Ranges from high class hotels to holiday cottages, bed and breakfast accommodation, to camp sites. Details from the tourist office.

Cable Cars and Chairlifts in the Area
Ahornbahn   Gschösswand lift
Penkenbahn   Rosenalm lift (Zell am Ziller)
Horbergbahn   Olperer glacier (above Hintertux)
Schrofenbahn   Gerlossteinalm lift

Recommended Local Excursions
Innsbruck   37 miles (60km) by rail or road to the north-west. Busy city with links with the Austro-Hungarian Empire. Museums, art galleries, buildings: Goldenes Dachl (Golden Roof) in Herzog Friedrich Strasse. Shops, restaurants, public gardens, cable car ascents into the Karwendel mountains.
Zell am Ziller   5 miles (8km) north. Steam train, shops, trout fishing.
Hintertux   11 miles (18km). Thermal swimming pool. All-year-round skiing facilities.

For guest cards, guided tours and walking badge scheme enquire at the local tourist office.

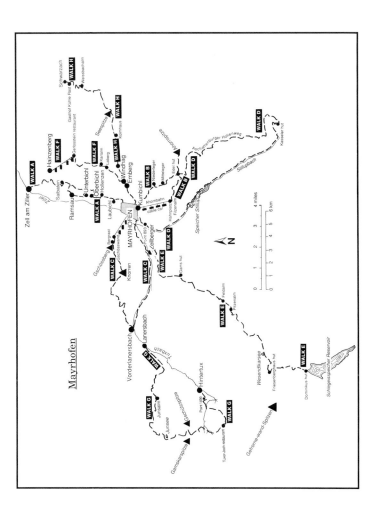

Mayrhofen

Schwarzach
WALK H
Wiesbachalm
Gasthof Kühe Rast
Gerlosstein restaurant
Hainzenberg
WALK F
Seegrube
WALK H
Kamlhaus
Kameiberg
WALK F
Kaniam
WALK H
Laberg
Windhag
WALK O
Emberg
Kiasseler hut
WALK B
Zell am Ziller
WALK A
Saibaten
Ramsau
WALK A
Unterbichl
Oberbichl
Hollenzen
Kumbichl
Niederseger
Mittelseger
Edel hut
Fügenberg
WALK B
Arondzipze
Aschaffenburger Hohenweg
WALK D
WALK B
Ziller
Laubichl
MAYRHOFEN
Point 893
Ahombahn
cable car
Hahnpalz
Stillupbach
Bergrast
Zeliberger
WALK D
Speicher Stillup
Geboidsberg
Sidóboden
WALK G
Knorren
WALK C
Görns hut
WALK C
N
0 1 2 3 4 miles
0 1 2 3 4 5 6 km
Vorderlanersbach
WALK D
Lanersbach
Tuxbach
Feldalm
WALK E
Penalm
Wesendikarsee
Hintertux
WALK G
Junsalm
Friesenberghaus hut
WALK E
Dominikus hut
Gschosspitze
Jursee
Gamskarspitze
Point 466
WALK G
Tuxer-Joch restaurant
Gefrome-wand Spitzen
Schlegelsspeicher Reservoir

94

A • ZELL AM ZILLER

5$\frac{1}{2}$ miles (9km). 2–3 hours. Easy.

This short easy valley walk is used as the opening route in the Mayrhofen area on the assumption that several days leading up to the holiday, have been spent travelling. If this is so, it is always an excellent idea to start with an easy walk — not only does it allow jaded muscles to tone up, but it also gives time to appreciate the area and get your bearings.

The route follows a pleasant woodland path down the valley, skirting the small village of Ramsau, where there is an optional diversion for coffee. Beyond Ramsau, the path climbs steeply, but easily through the forest, passing farmsteads built in small clearances within the forest, to join the Gerlos Pass road where it zigzags into the Ziller valley at Unterberg. The main road is easily avoided by the use of linking paths and rural lanes which work their way into Zell am Ziller.

On the return journey to Mayrhofen the choice of transport is either bus or train. If opting for the latter, it will mean a ride on the famous Zillertal narrow gauge steam train, an opportunity not to be missed, so check train times in advance and plan the walk accordingly.

The Route

1 ☐   The walk starts at the Europahaus, Mayrhofen's sports centre. Walk due east, uphill past modern houses and hotels to Durst.

2 ☐   Continue beyond the built-up area and aim for the forest edge.

3 ☐   Join a footpath and turn left, slightly downhill, continuing along the forest edge.

Pause above the town and admire its setting. The view to the west is directly along the narrow Tuxertal and the wooded slopes of Penken beckon upwards. Penken is an easy mountain to climb and the pause at this point could be used to plan a climb later in the holiday. For the actual route see the Penken walk (C).

4 ☐   Walk down the valley, passing the open fields surrounding Laubichl and the camp site.

5 ☐   Cross the portal of the tunnel built to take the new road, to bypass Mayrhofen.

6 ☐ Walk down to the village of Hollenzen.

7 ☐ Turn left into the village and right, by valley road through meadowland to Oberbichl.

8 ☐ Turn right along a lane to Unterbichl.

Many interesting old timber farm buildings line the roadside, or are on side tracks. It is worth stopping to look at the different styles of architecture, or to admire the massed geraniums and petunias in window boxes.

9 ☐ Either turn right and climb back uphill into the forest, bearing left at a junction of tracks, or continue ahead into Ramsau village for a coffee stop.

The baroque church in Ramsau is worth a visit.

10 ☐ From Ramsau follow the lane, east from the church, zigzagging uphill into the forest to join the track from Unterbichl.

11 ☐ Turn left along a track giving access to a series of hill farms and haybarns.

There is a good view of Penken — 6,876ft (2,095m) in the clearing below Saibaten.

12 ☐ Climb up to the farmsteads of Saibaten, by the signposted track.

13 ☐ On the northern edge of a clearing, turn right at a junction and follow a steep path uphill through the pine forest.

14 ☐ Turn left on a forest track, downhill at first, then follow the contours around the hillside and into an area of scrubby trees on a rocky hillside as far as the Gerlos Pass road.

15 ☐ At the road, turn left away from it on a path leading to a series of hill farms.

16 ☐ Bear right, back towards the road. Turn left on the road and walk round a hairpin bend, then left downhill on a path.

17 ☐ Cross the tunnel entrance to the Zell am Ziller bypass, then turn right on a minor road.

18 ☐ Walk past the camp site and into the outskirts of Zell am Ziller. Walk on into the town, the railway station is in the town centre.

B • AHORNSPITZE

8 miles (13km). 6–8 hours. Moderate/Strenuous.
3,499ft (1,066m) ascent. 7,596ft (2,315m) descent.

Even though half of the climb to Ahornspitze from Mayrhofen is gained by using the Ahornbahn cable car, there is still another 3,499ft (1,066m) to climb to the narrow summit of this attractive mountain. The way is steep and rocky and the final slopes can be covered in snow, so it is essential that walkers have a good head for heights and are adequately equipped; ie carrying an ice axe and be skilled in its use. It should be possible to hire ice axes locally in one of Mayrhofen's sports shops. If not, turn away and follow the walk downhill from the Edel hut, leaving a potentially dangerous route at a safe point. There will be another day and you will be alive to enjoy it!

From the Edel hut, the path again follows a steep route back down the rocky pine-covered hillside to a mountain farm at Niederleger. Beyond, the path enters the forest and drops steeply back into Mayrhofen.

The Route

1 ☐ Take the Ahornbahn cable car from Kumbichl (south from Mayrhofen town centre on the Zillergrund road), to its top station at Hahnplatz on the Filzenalm alp.

2 ☐ Follow the signposted path away from the upper station, across the rocky alpine pasture to a footpath junction. Turn left.

3 ☐ Follow the contours then climb gently around the north slope of the Filzenschneid ridge.

The rocky slopes of the Filzenschneid are a good area to look for alpine flowers.

4 ☐ Go round the head of a dry valley and climb to the Edel hut.

5 ☐ Five paths cross at the hut, take the eastern one, half right and signposted to the Ahornspitze.

Check conditions on the Ahornspitze before leaving the Edel hut.

6 ☐ Climb steadily up the grassy lower slopes of the peak, then on to its rocky upper limits.

A cross and maybe a visitors' book in a tin box mark the summit of the Ahornspitze — 9,757ft (2,973m). The view is magnificent. To the south is the Zillertaler Alpen group, its serrated ice- and snow-covered skyline marking the border between Italy and Austria. To the east is the Glockner range, home of Austria's highest summit, and to the north and west are all the Tyrolean giants.

7 ☐ Return, taking care on the steep descent of the rocky western slopes as far as the Edel hut and well earned refreshment.

The Edel hut offers several possibilities. It could be used for an overnight stay in the mountains, or simply for a meal. All are welcome, but members of the Austrian Alpine Club are given preferential rates for overnight accommodation. The other alternative is in the choice of route. The walk down is steep so if anyone is feeling tired, then an easy option would be to walk back to Filzenalm and take the cable car.

8 ☐ Walk steeply downhill from the hut through a boulder field as far as the upper limits of the pine forest.

9 ☐ Follow the forest edge to the left past an old hill farm at Mitteleger.

10 ☐ Join an access track and turn left through the hill settlement of Niederleger.

It may be possible to buy refreshment in Niederleger at the Wirthaus Alpenrose.

11 ☐ Bear left downhill across the clearing below Niederleger and enter the pine forest.

12 ☐ Zigzag steeply downhill through the forest. Go past a wayside shrine usually decorated with flowers and pine boughs.

13 ☐ Cross a small river and join a forest road, continuing downhill.

14 ☐ At a junction with a surfaced road, turn right, then immediately left, around a sharp bend. Follow the road through Kumbichl and into Mayrhofen.

C • PENKEN

5¹/₂ miles (9km). 4–5 hours. Moderate.

Penken — 6,876ft (2,095m) makes a very pleasant high-level excursion. By using the Gschösswand lift as a direct ascent from Mayrhofen, most of the day can be spent above the tree line. All the high-level section of the walk is on a narrow, but safe, ridge giving the mountaineer a genuine feeling of being above the rest of his fellow men. If the weather is kind, the day will be spent in enjoyable sunshine — which is always stronger at a higher altitude than in the lower valleys.

The route starts immediately above the tree line and climbs the broad shoulder of Gschössberg, where most of the steep climbing ends. An easier angle leads to Penken, not the highest point on the walk, but certainly the most dramatically situated. A narrowing rocky ridge leads to Wangalm and the end of high-level walking for the day. The downhill path is steep at first, but the angle eases on reaching the tree line again, where an easy track makes its way into the village of Vorderlanersbach.

The Route

1 ☐   Use the Gschösswand cable to reach its upper station at 5,783ft (1,762m).

2 ☐   Follow the central of three tracks radiating from the lift. Climb easily to Bergrast restaurant.

Pause to admire the views opposite of the magnificent range of mountains and glaciers which make both the skyline and the Austro/Italian frontier.

3 ☐   Start to climb more steeply towards the bottom station of a ski-lift.

4 ☐   Take a right fork on a path away from the track and climb the scrubby hillside alongside the ski-lift cable.

5 ☐   Reach the summit of Gschössberg, the eastern end of the Penken ridge.

6 ☐   Follow the path, along a broad ridge through an area of scrub and rock-covered hillocks.

High-level walking above Mayrhofen

---

7 ☐ Continue uphill to the top of Penken's prominent summit.

8 ☐ Bear right, slightly downhill. Ignore the path diverging to the left.

9 ☐ Follow the narrow undulating ridge to the Wangalm col.

There is a good view to the south-west, along the upper reaches of the Tuxertal valley.

10 ☐ Go left, steeply downhill, away from the upper station of the ski-lift. Follow the rocky path down the steep spur as far as the junction with an access track. Turn left onto the track.

11 ☐ Follow the zigzag route of the track to a quarry and turn left, away from a group of buildings.

12 ☐   Slant down the hillside to a group of summer farms and a tiny mountain chapel.

13 ☐   Go right away from the chapel on a path which then enters the upper limits of a pine wood.

14 ☐   On an easing gradient, go downhill, through the pines and cross a cleared stretch dotted with barns and small farms.

15 ☐   Re-enter the forest and pass a series of carved trees.

16 ☐   Join a forest track and follow it across steep sloping hillside hay meadows into Vorderlanersbach.

There should be ample opportunity to buy refreshments before moving on from Vorderlanersbach.

17 ☐   Either follow the valley road downhill back to Mayrhofen, or to save the effort, wait for the post bus or arrange to be taken by taxi.

D • KASSELER HUT VIA THE ASCHAFFENBURGER HÖHENWEG

21 miles (34km). 9–10 hours. Strenuous.

While this may seem a long walk to be undertaken in a mountainous environment, it does not have many great changes in height. In fact, for most of the high-level section, the path, a delightful belvedere, is mostly downhill beneath a snow-topped ridge, which runs north from Stagenspitz on the Italian border. This is the Aschaffenburger Höhenweg, a famous high-level mountain track. The path ends at the Kasseler hut beneath Östliches Stillupkees glacier. A steep path leads into the Stillup valley where a long, but gradually improving track, leads down to a reservoir, the Speicher Stillup, and eventually into the main valley at Mayrhofen.

Even though there are no great technical difficulties involved in this walk, it must be remembered that it is long and therefore tiring. Take plenty of liquid for the open mountain sides where dehydration of the body can be a major problem. In case of emergency, an overnight stop could be made at the Kasseler hut, which could be used to spread the long walk over 2 days. Another alternative method of shortening the walk, would be to arrange for transport to pick you up somewhere in the Stillup valley.

The Route

1 ☐ Reach Filzenalm by the Ahornbahn cable car from Kumbichl.

2 ☐ Follow the signposted path around the rocky shoulder of the Filzenschneid ridge to reach the Edel hut.

3 ☐ Turn right, to the south, away from the hut and climb the steep rocky hillside to the summit of Toreggenkopf — 8,107ft (2,470m).

A pause for breath will be essential on top of Toreggenkopf, fortunately at the end of the steepest climb of the day. Directly downhill and in front is a reservoir, the Speicher Stillup, to be seen at close quarters later in the day, near the end of the walk.

4 ☐ Go steadily downhill on the footpath, the Aschaffenburger Höhenweg, following it across a series of wide rocky corries and climbing their dividing ridges along the way.

The west-facing corries are an alpine flower-lover's paradise. Many varieties can be seen along the way, but remember they are protected and even collecting their blooms is forbidden.

5 ☐ The path gradually loses height until, on rounding the Rosswand ridge and entering the Sonntagskar corrie, it climbs uphill for the last time to pass a rock slide.

6 ☐ Go steeply downhill towards the steep west ridge of Hintere Stangenspitze at the foot of which is the Kasseler hut.

Think carefully before leaving the hut. Unless transport has been arranged to meet you somewhere along the Stillup vallley, or everyone is capable of finishing the walk in one day, serious consideration should be given to spending a night in the comfort and safety of the Kasseler hut.

7 ☐ Turn right away from the hut and go very steeply downhill on a rocky path. Cross a small stream and enter a scrubby pine forest.

8 ☐ Walk beneath taller trees into the valley bottom.

9 ☐ Follow the river downstream, keeping above its rocky floodbed.

An alpine farm

Tiny alpine farmsteads passed along the way, are used only in summer. Refreshments will usually be available at several farms and huts in the valley.

10 ☐   On an improving track, follow the east bank of the Speicher Stillup.

In the right light conditions and on a windless day, it should be possible to use the reservoir's still waters to photograph reflections of the border peaks lining the valley head.

11 ☐   Join the access road and follow it down the eastern side of the dam wall.

Look back at the dam to appreciate its strength.

12 ☐   Follow the road through the narrow forested gorge.

13 ☐   Either continue by road into Kumbichl or turn left at point 893 and follow a steep signposted path downhill through the forest into Mayrhofen.

E • THE BERLINER HÖHENWEG

12$\frac{1}{2}$ miles (20km). 7 hours. Moderate.

The Berliner Höhenweg is a high-level contour-hugging path, which starts with a long, straightforward climb from the dam of a reservoir, the Schlegeisspeicher. The path is well maintained and walking is easy, once the initial climb has been completed. With the exception of a short section at the beginning and a slightly longer one at the end, the path is more or less above the tree line all the way. As it faces the south-east, the path will be in constant sunshine, so wear light, protective clothing.

The best way to do the Berliner Höhenweg is either to take the post bus or arrange for a mini bus or taxi to make a special journey as far as the reservoir (arrange this through the tourist office in Mayrhofen). The early part of the walk is spent on climbing to the Freisenberghaus hut. From here the route is easy, following the contours north-east above the valley as far as the Gams hut, then downhill to Zellberger and the road back to Mayrhofen.

The Route

1 ☐   Use either the post bus or other transport to reach the Schlegeisspeicher — 5,924ft (1,805m). The walk starts from the Dominikus hut restaurant at the west side of the massive concrete dam.

2 ☐   Follow the signposted path to the north, through a pine forest and into the Lapenkarbach valley.

3 ☐   Turn left upstream, crossing and recrossing as dictated by the rocky path.

There will be a good view of the reservoir once you climb above the tree line.

4 ☐   Climb the final combe to reach the welcome sight of the Friesenberghaus hut — 8,130ft (2,477m), and its tiny lake.

The snowclad peak above the lake and to the west of the hut is the Gefrorne-Wand-Spitzen — 10,791ft (3,288m) an area of all-year skiing.

5 ☐   Leave the hut and follow the signposted path, the Berliner

Höhenweg, eastwards on a level path around the broad south-facing spur from the Peterskopfl. Ignore a path diverging right.

6 ☐ Pass the attractive Wesendlkarsee, this lake making an ideal resting place and viewpoint.

7 ☐ The path continues to the north-east, more or less level all the way to Pitzenalm, a mountain farmstead.

8 ☐ Go through an area of scrubby pine forest to Feldalm.

9 ☐ Take the left-hand fork at Feldalm and climb the open hillside, steep in places, to a col on a side ridge between the main ridge and Wildschrofen.

10 ☐ Begin to descend gradually and then cross an area of steep rocky slopes above the tree line.

The views from the path are beyond compare. Remember to stop frequently and look back, both along the path and across the valley towards the snow-covered frontier peaks.

11 ☐ Walk steeply downhill from a path junction to the welcoming shade of the Gams hut.

12 ☐ Follow the signposted and well used path downhill from the hut, along a specially cleared area used as a ski-run in winter.

13 ☐ At the bottom station of the ski-lift, turn right on an access track; follow it through mature pine forest as far as the road at Zellberger.

14 ☐ Walk down to the main Tuxertal road above Furkenberg and either catch the bus or walk the $2^3/_4$ miles (4km) back to Mayrhofen.

F • GERLOSSTEIN

5 miles (8km). 3 hours. Easy.

Assuming the previous walks have been followed in succession, this walk is included in the itinerary as a rest, following harder walks over more open and higher ground.

More or less downhill all the way from the top of the Gerlossteinalm lift, this walk enjoys the shade of pine forests throughout its length.

The route is south across an area of steep hillsides, but uses cleverly designed paths which follow easy contours around shoulders and through tree-clad corries all the way back to Mayrhofen.

The Route

1 □   Take the bus to Zell am Ziller and then change on to the Gerlos Pass bus. Take this as far as Hainzenberg.

2 □   Use the cableway to reach the Gerlosstein mountain restaurant.

3 □   Turn right away from the restaurant along its access road for about 40yd (37m) and turn left at a fork.

4 □   Take the track across open hillside and through short stretches of forest, following the contours round to the mountain farm at Kotahornalm.

5 □   Walk ahead on a footpath, gently uphill and into dense pine forest.

6 □   Follow a level path through the forest to the cleared land and grazing of Karlalm.

7 □   Follow the contours across a scrub-covered hillside and then go down to Laberg farmstead.

8 □   Bear right, steeply downhill into the Kasernwald forest. Continue on this path as far as a mountain road. Bear right again and then left, to reach the scattered village of Windhag.

9 □   At a junction, take the track on the right, to Emberg.

10 □   Beyond the last of the houses, bear left, steeply downhill on a zigzag path through the forest to Mayrhofen.

G • GAMSKARSPITZE AND JUNSBACHTAL

11 miles (18km). 8–9 hours. Very strenuous.
4,125ft (1,257m) ascent.

The narrow, steep-sided Tuxertal climbs high above the flat-bottomed Zillertal, and it is inhabited almost as far as the foot of the massive Tuxer glacier which marks its upper limits. Hintertux, its last village, is bustling, but free from too many tourists and is used as a base for all-year-round skiing on the nearby glaciers. Thermal springs provide natural hot water for relaxing swimming pools in the village.

The walk begins at Hintertux and quickly gains height by a series of paths and tracks to reach the welcome respite of the col at TuxerJoch and its restaurant. The ridge to the north is beyond the capabilities of most hillwalkers, so a little of the height is lost, before starting a steep, hard climb to the summit of Gschützspitze, the eastern satellite of Gamskarspitze — 9,025ft (2,750m). A steady traverse, going up and downhill as dictated by the mountainsides, crosses the slopes below the wall of mountains marking the western rim of the Tuxer valley. Junsjoch — 8,152ft (2,484m) marks the end of the climbing and the way is then steeply downhill into the Tuxer valley and the road with its bus service.

The Route

1 ☐   Take the bus to Hintertux (check times and other details of the service at the Mayrhofen tourist office).

2 ☐   Walk along the valley road, past a ski-tow and as far as a farmhouse on the right dominated by a hillside cross. Turn right and climb through hay meadows to the edge of a pine forest.

3 ☐   At a junction with a forest road, turn left along the track as far as the junction of four paths and tracks. Turn left on a narrow lane.

4 ☐   Leave the upper limits of the forest and cross a rocky hillside.

There should be plenty of alpine flowers on the slopes above the forest and a good view of the Tuxertal and its glaciers.

5 ☐   Turn right away from the track on a well made path climbing by the side of a mountain stream.

6 ☐ Bear right at another path junction and climb to the prominent col of the Tuxer-Joch.

Do not stay too long in the Tuxer-Joch restaurant — there is a long hard day ahead.

7 ☐ Turn right at the col, downhill across the upper combe and follow the left bank of the Weitentalbach.

8 ☐ Left at a path junction and climb steeply uphill to the small col between Gschützspitze and its taller neighbour the Gamskarspitze.

If time and energy allows, a climb of Gamskarspitze, to the left, by its narrow east ridge is recommended.

9 ☐ Downhill across the rocky upper slopes of the Jensbach valley.

10 ☐ Ahead at a path junction and climb above the tiny lake of Junssee. Cross a minor col at Pluderling.

11 ☐ Bear right, downhill below the slopes of Geier and cross the headwaters of a mountain stream.

12 ☐ Climb steeply to the Junsbach col.

13 ☐ Go steeply downhill on a rocky path into the Junsbach valley and turn left at a path junction by the hill farm of Junsalm.

14 ☐ Follow the farm access track above the left bank of the stream. The lower sections of the track are in the welcome shade of pine forest.

Tiny wayside shrines decorated with alpine flowers attract the eye.

15 ☐ Go left at a track junction and follow an easy angled route along the lower edge of the forest.

16 ☐ Go through hay meadows into Lanersbach to catch the bus.

H • BRANDBERGERJOCH

9 miles (14km). 8 hours. Strenuous. 3,662ft (1,116m) ascent.

Brandbergerjoch Pass — 7,572ft (2,307m) marks the lowest gap in a long ridge above the Zillergrund valley; it starts as a narrow, almost knife-edge arrêt, the south-west ridge of the Zillerkopf — 9,830ft (2,995m), the valley's main mountain. From the top of the pass the view seems to cover almost the whole of the Austrian Tyrol. In the south, the frontier ridge extends roughly east–west as a line of snow clad peaks, whilst closer to hand is the long rocky ridge climbing towards the Zillerkopf. Below it is a deep tree-lined trough of Ziller-grund and behind, in the direction of the start of the walk, is the Gerlos Pass, one of Austria's passes which are open all year round.

From the Gerlos road, the path starts from the conveniently sited Kühle *Gasthof.* It then climbs steeply through a hillside clearing and past a series of mountain farms used only in summer, before reaching, by a rough and rocky hillside, the narrow gap of the Brandbergerjoch. Beyond, the route is downhill all the way to the tree line and an alpine village which will provide a pleasant diversion before starting on the last short, steep descent into the main valley.

The Route

1 ☐   Take the Gerlos Pass post bus from Zell am Ziller to the Gasthof Kühle Rast about half way up the pass.

2 ☐   Continue along the road for about a third of a mile (536m) and turn right on a side track along the western edge of a forest clearing.

3 ☐   Cross a small stream and turn left to follow it upstream ignoring a side track along the forest edge.

4 ☐   Walk uphill to a group of farm buildings.

5 ☐   Turn right behind the uppermost group of barns and zigzag to the right around a steep hillside. Skirt the edge of the pine forest.

6 ☐   Go past the farmstead at Weissbachalm and in and out of side arms of the forest. Follow the hillside above the stream, the Weiss-bachl.

7 ☐   Continue uphill on a zigzag path.

Pause above the last farm to admire the view northwards of central Tyrol.

8 ☐   Clamber down to and cross the stream. Follow the opposite bank upstream to a footpath junction. Ignore the path diverging right and continue upstream.

Notice how the varieties of alpine flowers change with the decreasing moisture away from the stream. Globeflowers, primulas and mosses almost sit in the water, but further away are the less water-tolerant plants such as saxifrages and gentian.

9 ☐   Cross the stream and climb a rocky spur to reach a tiny pool; it has no name, but the nearby hill is called the Seespitze.

All pools and lakes are known as 'see' in German, no matter how small or large they may be.

10 ☐   Reach the top of the Brandbergerjoch.

It goes without saying that you will want to take a rest at the top of the pass. The pool will be a tempting spot to cool tired feet. Mountains range on all sides and the view makes the climb worthwhile.

11 ☐   Go downhill from the pass towards a rocky stream bed. Follow it, passing clumps of scrubby pines until you reach the small farmstead of Kolmhaus.

12 ☐   Bear right out of the valley, downhill towards the dense pine-forested lower slopes. Ignore a more level path on the right.

13 ☐   Go through the hamlet of Ahornbach and follow its access track down to the track junction at Windhag. Continue towards Emberg.

It should be possible to find refreshments at one of the hillside hamlets along the way.

14 ☐   From Emberg, go steeply downhill on a zigzag path through the forest and into the outskirts of Mayrhofen.

6 NEUKIRCHEN

Map

Kompass Wanderkarte (1:50,000 series) Sheet 38; Venediger-gruppe Oberpinzgau.

How to Get There

Road

South-east by the European motorway system to Munich. Continue along the Salzburg *Autobahn* as far as the Rosenheim interchange. Then south and enter Austria at Kufstein. Road 173 to St Johann in Tirol, then 170 to Kitzbühel, or from Wörgl take road 170 via Brixen to Kitzbühel. South over the Thurn Pass to Mittersill, then west along the valley road to Neukirchen.

Rail

Main line Trans-European services via either Salzburg or Innsbruck to Wörgl. Branch line via St Johan in Tirol and Zell am See. West along the Salzach valley line.

Air

Either Salzburg or Innsbruck by scheduled airlines and rail as above.

The Area

According to a bust in a tiny formal garden in the town centre, Emperor Franz Joseph, the last emperor to preside over the final days of the colossal Austro-Hungarian Empire, was an admirer of Neukirchen. He made frequent visits to this sunny place, no doubt as an escape from more formal life at court in Vienna.

Neukirchen is about halfway along the upper section of the Salzach valley, a broad, lush valley running east from its dramatic beginnings at the foot of the Krimml Falls. To the north are the Kitzbüheler Alps, and south as far as the Austro-Italian frontier stretch the snow-clad peaks of the Venediger group and Austria's highest summit, the Grossglockner — literally the 'Great Bell'.

Because of the formation and comparatively low height of the mountains, hillwalking is easier to the north of the Salzach valley. To the south, long valley walks are necessary for anyone wanting to reach the giants of the border range. Well situated mountain huts in the valleys and around the southern peaks offer friendly hospitality to anyone exploring these wild regions. Even though the Salzach valley is only a few miles from the Zillertal, and linked by a modern motor road across the Gerlos Pass, the two valleys are entirely different and developed from times when travel was essentially on foot or horse-back, often along dangerous tracks. Guarded passes were once important barriers against intruders. Schloss Mittersill, the castle at the foot of the Thurn Pass to the east, commanded all traffic entering and leaving the middle valley. The building is well preserved and today is an exclusive hotel catering mainly for hunting parties. The village church was 'new' (for that is the translation of Neukirchen) around 1500 and is in the usual rococo style associated with Austria. Of particular note are the baroque pulpit and the Krausen chapel with its delightful Madonna and child statue.

Industry in the area is essentially geared to tourism, but farming is still very strong, albeit on the small scale made necessary in alpine areas. Copper was extensively mined nearby and traces of the old furnaces and stamp mills can still be found around the local hillsides. The industry died out in the middle of the nineteenth century.

As the Salzach valley runs roughly east–west, villages on its northern hillsides enjoy the maximum hours of sunshine. This, to-gether with the many facilities on offer, ranging from concerts, bird watching, alpine flowers, golf, ten-pin bowling, or simply soaking up the sun and alpine atmosphere, makes Neukirchen worth considera-tion by groups and families who might be divided on the merits or otherwise of an alpine walking holiday. Ease of access to good roads connecting places like Innsbruck and Salzburg, comes high on the list of inducements to the area.

Mention must be made of the Hohe Tauern National Park. The park encloses all the mountains between the Salzach valley and the Austro-Italian border, stretching eastwards from the Reichenspitze in Sudtirol (South Tyrol); taking in the Grossvenediger and Grossglock-ner peaks and ending at the Gasterntal in the east.

One chairlift serves the southern slopes of the Wildkogel, Neukirchen's own 'mountain'. With the aid of this lift it is possible to make a number of high-level walks across the grassy slopes and ridges of this sunny plateau, which is an ideal vantage point for views of the higher peaks to the south. Rail and post bus services can be used to reach points up or down the valley and so extend the range of walking possibilities.

Useful Information

Local Tourist Office
Verkehrsverein Neukirchen
A-5741 Neukirchen am Grossvenediger
☎ 06565-6256

Accommodation
The usual range from alpine resort hotels to holiday cottages, bed and breakfast accommodation. Camp sites nearby at Krimml, Wald, Weyer, Hollersbach and Mittersill.

Cable Cars and Chairlifts in the Area
Wildkogel   Double chairlift. Bottom station to the east of Neukirchen town centre.
Resterhöhe   Chairlift, from the summit of the Thurn Pass (road), to the Gasthof Resterhöhe. (Winter only).
Plattenkogel   Chairlift from the Gasthof Filzenheim to the east of the Gerlos Pass.

Recommended Local Excursions
Innsbruck   By road to the north-west. Shops, museums, art galleries. Railway links with mainline services throughout Europe.
Salzburg   By road or rail. Shops, restaurants, churches, cathedral, castle, formal gardens, concerts. Links with Mozart.
Schloss Hohenneukirchen: Twelfth-century castle to the north of the town centre. Favoured as a country retreat by Emperor Franz Joseph. Check locally for opening times.

For guest card facilities, guided walks, walking badge scheme check details with the local tourist office.

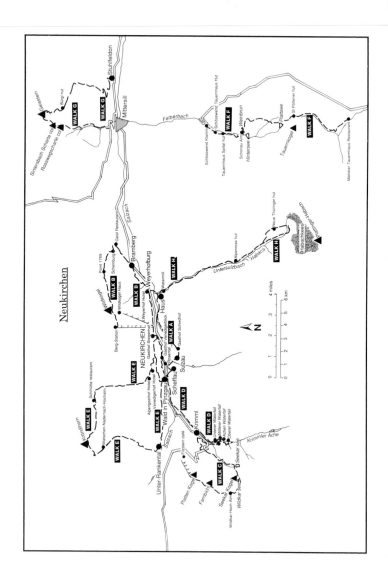

Neukirchen

114

A • AROUND NEUKIRCHEN

$5^1/_2$ miles (9km). 3 hours. Easy.

Here is an ideal way of both getting to know the shops and facilities of Neukirchen and the varied countryside surrounding the town.

The route uses a series of linked footpaths and wanders through quiet forest glades and open meadows on either side of the Salzach valley. It also gives a glimpse of one of the north-facing side valleys draining the massive peaks of the Venediger range; this valley, the Obersulzbachtal is crossed in its lowest reaches and should give an indication of the attractions further south and upstream. Easy river-side tracks follow the main river as far as Habachtal, arguably the finest of the three valleys either crossed or followed on this walk. Crossing the main valley for a second time near Weyer, a field path along the lower edge of the Hohenbramberg forest, leads back to Neukirchen.

The Route

1 □   The walk starts in front of the *Rathaus* (town hall) in the town centre. Walk westwards along the main shopping street as far as a crossroads.

2 □   Continue ahead through the outskirts of Neukirchen to a 'T' junction.

3 □   Follow the footpath, which continues ahead and across the road at the junction and beyond the tennis courts. This path is not shown on some maps, but is signposted as path No 10 and Fitness Parcours.

4 □   Climb the forested slope for about 100yd (90m).

5 □   Keep right at a footpath junction, continuing to climb uphill through pine forest.

6 □   Cross the broad ridge and descend, still in pine forest towards the Durnbach valley.

7 □   Join the road at the crossroads above the Sauglbrücke bridge.

8 □   Turn left along the road and over the bridge.

9 ☐ Immediately over the bridge, turn left on a forest road which should be signposted as path No 13. Follow this as far as the main valley road at the Gasthof Venedigerblick.

The Venedigerblick restaurant should make a timely coffee stop.

10 ☐ Go right at the main road to walk through the scattered hamlet of Rosental.

11 ☐ Opposite a wayside chapel at the side of the Gasthof Burgfeld, turn left away from the main road and walk down a narrow lane.

12 ☐ Cross the railway to the right of a small station.

13 ☐ Cross the river by a bridge and turn left at a triple fork next to a group of farm buildings.

14 ☐ Walk across meadowland as far as the river, the Obersulzbach.

The view to the south over the flower-filled meadow is of the rocky and snow-covered peaks of the Venediger range, which rise above the pine-clad slopes of the lower mountains.

15 ☐ Walk on and into Sulzau village.

There is a restaurant, the Gasthof Steigerhof in Sulzau.

16 ☐ Turn right and walk a little way through the village, then look out for a signposted path on the left beyond Gasthof Steigerhof.

17 ☐ Go left on a field path towards a group of buildings and the Gasthof Schiedhof.

18 ☐ Left along the access road, then right, crossing the Untersulzbach to follow its right-hand bank, downstream.

19 ☐ Where the stream joins the main Salzach river, turn right along a minor road to follow the river downstream.

20 ☐ Do not cross the river, but continue to follow it, still downstream, on a path along its built-up south bank.

21 ☐ Cross two more roads still walking downstream.

22 ☐ Move away from the river, through lush meadowland to join the Habachtal road below the hamlet of Haus. Turn left.

The snow-clad mountains near Neukirchen

23 □   Go over both the river and the railway and walk up to the main road.

24 □   Bear right, then leave the road at the first lane on the left. Walk towards the Weyerhof Hotel.

25 □   Do not pass the hotel, but turn left on a field track which becomes a footpath beyond a couple of farm buildings.

26 □   Follow the path and eventually a minor road along the lower edge of pine forest back to Neukirchen.

B • WILDKOGEL

8¹/₂ miles (14km). 5–6 hours. Moderate.
4,490ft (1,368m) descent.

Most of this walk is spent above the tree line on the relatively broad upper slopes of the Wildkogel 7,302ft (2,225m). This is an easy mountain to climb, because the initial 4,076ft (1,242m) are gained by using the double chairlift from Neukirchen. The scramble over the final rocky summit of the Wildkogel is relatively easy and the descent towards the tree line is simplicity itself.

The mountain is a place to savour, the views are magnificent and closer to hand, or more correctly at foot, are thousands of alpine flowers with colours ranging from bright yellow to scarlet and blue.

The open section of the walk ends at the Wetterkreuz, where forest closes the view, but on a hot day its shade will probably come as a welcome relief. A steep path leads down through the forest to ·reach the open meadows above Obermühlbach where the Geisl restaurant will make a welcome diversion. A quiet road leads on to Bramberg where farm lanes and field paths wander through lush pasture towards Neukirchen.

Anyone who has found the descent a little tiring can take the bus from Bramberg.

The Route

1 ☐   Use the double chairlift from Neukirchen to reach the Berg-station on the western upper slopes of Wildkogel.

Pause to admire the view to the south which takes in the Grossvenediger mountains on the far side of the Salzach valley. To the north and close at hand, are the lesser but still attractive Kitzbüheler Alps.

2 ☐   Turn right away from the upper station and climb the broad, grassy shoulder.

Spend time looking for alpine flowers. Many of the smaller and less obvious plants are more attractive when viewed at close range. Larger flowers such as alpenrose, anemones and gentians also flourish on the shaly soil.

3 ☐   Ignore a path on the right which drops down to the Wildkogel Haus.

4 ☐   Cross a minor summit and go down into a shallow col which marks the junction of four paths. Continue ahead.

5 ☐   Climb the final shaly slopes to the top of the Wildkogel.

Regain your breath by admiring the all-round view from the summit cross.

6 ☐   Go steadily downhill for a little over 2 miles (3km) along a wide grassy ridge.

7 ☐   Climb slightly and cross the final summit on this ridge, the Wetterkreuz.

8 ☐   Go downhill towards the upper edge of the pine forest.

9 ☐   Enter the forest at point 1769 and follow the steep path downhill, using zigzags to ease the angle of descent.

10 ☐   Leave the forest at the group of farm buildings known as Schelnburg. Turn left at a junction a little way beyond the last barn.

11 ☐   Turn right on an access track and walk down to the Geisl restaurant.

12 ☐   Follow the access road down to Bramberg.

If ending the walk at Bramberg the bus stop is on the slip road, above the main road and to the east of the village.

13 ☐   Follow a quiet road through meadowland to Weichseldorf and then down through a series of fields to join a minor road by the side of the Weyerbach.

14 ☐   Follow the road into Weyerhofburg.

15 ☐   Use the field path beyong the Weyerhof restaurant to return to Neukirchen.

C • SEEKAR KOGEL

5 miles (8km). 5–6 hours. Moderate/Strenuous.
1,887ft (575m) ascent. 5,107ft (1,556m) descent.

Climbing the Seekar Kogel makes a delightful expedition, especially for anyone not normally used to scaling mountain peaks. There are no great technical difficulties, but nevertheless, as with all mountains, care and attention must be given to the ground underfoot at all times. Never make a move unless the next one is clear and never run, or even walk directly downhill.

Most of the height required in this walk is gained quickly by using the Platten Kogel chairlift from Filzstein, above the Gerlos Pass. Initially the terrain is undulating, but a contour-hugging path soon crosses the western slopes of the north ridge of the Seekar Kogel. At a group of farm buildings on Wildkar-Hoch Alm, the path divides and the steepest part of the walk is from there uphill to the Seekar Scharte, a col marked by a tiny lake. The summit of Seekar Kogel is only a matter of 312ft (95m) higher and therefore makes an interesting little scramble away from the path. The descent, to the north-east towards Krimml is steep and at first over rocky ground, easing as the path enters the forest above the village.

This walk may be extended by continuing down the Salzach valley using the route described in the next walk.

The Route

1 ☐   Take the Gerlos Pass post bus to the Filzstein café at Vorder-platte.

2 ☐   Use the chairlift to reach Platten Kogel — 6,692ft (2,039m).

There is a very pleasant view of the Salzach valley to the east and the Gerlos Pass to the north-west of the summit.

3 ☐   Walk southwards downhill across a broad grassy col.

4 ☐   Turn half right at the junction of four paths and go slightly downhill and around the wooded slopes of Farnbichl 6,656ft (2,028m).

5 ☐   Climb slightly along the western limits of the scrubby trees; keep ahead at a path junction.

The Krimmler Achental

6 ☐   Follow the contours across the rocky hillside.

The slopes of the Seekar Kogel are home ground for marmots whose cheeky whistle indicates their presence. Alpine flowers also fill every crevice and sunny hollow.

7 ☐   Cross a small stream and walk towards the group of farm buildings at Wildkar-Hoch Alm and fork right.

8 ☐   Climb steeply and cross a second stream.

9 ☐   Continue uphill on rocky ground, gaining 1,703ft (519m) in about three-quarters of a mile (1km).

On the col, pause to admire the tiny Wildkar See before completing the climb.

10 ☐   Follow the rocky ridge north to the summit of the Seekar Kogel — 8,579ft (2,614m).

Camera enthusiasts will revel in the all-round views from this delightful mountain top.

11 ☐   Return to the lake and continue along the path, in a north-

easterly direction, steeply downhill over a steep boulder field.

12 ☐   Cross a small stream below the outflow of the Seekar See.

13 ☐   Turn left at a footpath junction and follow the east bank of the stream as far as the forested slopes above Krimml.

14 ☐   Cross the stream and continue to walk downhill.

15 ☐   Move away from the stream above a rocky outcrop, still following the footpath.

16 ☐   Cross the busy main road with care and follow the well made path on its far side into Krimml village.

17 ☐   Either return by post bus, or join the Krimml walk by turning right to follow a signposted path as far as the Krimml waterfall and then use the instructions for that walk.

D • THE KRIMML WATERFALL

$6^1/_2$ miles (10km). 3 hours. Easy.

As mentioned in the previous walk, this one is intended to be a continuation of that route, for those with energy to spare after the steep climb over the Seekar Kogel. It also makes a suitable half-day's excursion on days when either the weather, inclination, or other activities prevent longer expeditions.

The Krimml Falls are southern Europe's highest, and their spectacular setting, in a deeply wooded gorge, have justifiably made them a major tourist attraction. Starting from the roadside in Krimml village, the route at first is by the valley road along the river, the Krimmler Ache, as far as the Oberer (upper) Falls. It is necessary to retrace the route to reach a narrow footbridge and gain a footpath which skirts the more dramatic Achen and Mittlerer (middle) Falls. A little further and Unterer (lower) Falls are reached. Woodland paths link with each other along the south, or right-hand bank of the Salzach river as far as Neukirchen.

The Route

1 ☐   Take the train or post bus to Krimml.

The Krimml Falls

2 □   From the camp site, follow the road south and go under the main road.

3 □   Follow the Krimmler valley road (closed to all but essential traffic) uphill past three *Gasthöfe* for a little over $1^1/_4$ miles (2km).

4 ☐ Cross a side stream which runs down the Wasserfall Klamm and continue to walk as far as the next bend in the road. The Oberer Fall is on the left.

5 ☐ Retrace the route, downhill for about a third of a mile (0.5km) and look for a signposted path on the right.

6 ☐ Turn left and follow the path along the east (right) bank of the river, at first through meadowland, then into forest.

7 ☐ Pass the Achen and Mittlerer Falls, taking care on the rocky path.

8 ☐ The narrow rocky gorge forces the path away from the river above the final waterfall, the Unterer. It swings away then back to follow the riverbank around the outskirts of Krimml village.

9 ☐ Follow the river and keep to its southern bank as close as possible, ignoring any side paths.

10 ☐ Below the village of Wald, turn away uphill from the river.

11 ☐ At Scheffau turn left by a small church and follow the access lane as far as the railway.

12 ☐ Turn right across broad meadows on either side of the Salzbach and walk through the scattered houses of the hamlet of Sulzau.

13 ☐ Continue through fields to the Schiedhof restaurant, a good place to pause on the way home.

14 ☐ Do not follow the access road, but go half-right along a track, away from the restaurant and alongside the Untersulzbach. Follow this stream as far as the railway line.

15 ☐ Cross the railway and follow the most convenient of several tracks and minor roads into Neukirchen.

E • KRÖNDLHORN

13 miles (21km). 8–9 hours. Strenuous.
5,208ft (1,587m) ascent.

This is a tough walk, suitable for hard walkers, one where the rewards for the effort involved in the climb come with the marvellous view from the summit.

The route starts from and returns to Neukirchen, but could be shortened by using the bus or train back from Vorder-Krimml.

At the start of the walk, quiet roads lead into the upper section of the densely wooded Trattenbach valley, passing the conveniently sited Schihütte restaurant along the way. An open hillside above the riverhead is climbed by using a well designed path which wanders between rocky crags to the summit of the Kröndlhorn.

The downhill route at first is by way of the Nadernajoch, then down the stream, the Nadernachbach, as far as the old Gerlos Pass road. This road is followed as far as Wald in Pinzgau where field paths lead back to Neukirchen.

The Route

1 □   From Neukirchen town centre follow the Hohenneukirchen road westwards and uphill.

2 □   Go past the Venedigerhof and Alpengasthof Rechtegg hotels.

3 □   Leave the road at a sharp bend to the right and continue ahead on a forest road.

4 □   Climb steadily through dense pine forest above the east bank of the Trattenbach.

5 □   At a clearing in the forest, cross over to the opposite side of the river.

6 □   Climb the wooded hillside in front.

7 □   Cross the river again and climb up to the Schihütte restaurant.

The hut marks the limits of continuous forest. Above on the rocky hillside, trees become scrubbier.

8 □   Follow the stream along its north bank, uphill.

9 ☐ Bear right away from the stream and follow the path up the steep rocky hillside.

10 ☐ Climb to the summit cross on Kröndlhorn — 8,018ft (2,444m).

Pause to admire the panoramic all-round view from the top of the mountain.

11 ☐ Walk steeply downhill, to the south-west, as far as the broad col at Nadernajoch — 6,884ft (2,098m).

12 ☐ Bear left, downhill, to a group of summer farms at Watschen-Nadernach-Hochalm which sits on a grassy spur above the confluence of two small streams.

13 ☐ Follow the east, or left-hand side of the Nadernachbach to a second group of hill farms.

14 ☐ Still on the eastern (left) side of the stream, join a rough road and follow it down to the tree line.

15 ☐ Where the road bears right to cross the stream, walk ahead, away from the road still above the east bank of the stream.

16 ☐ Join another rough road and use this to reach the old Gerlos Pass road at Unter-Rankental.

17 ☐ Turn left along the road and follow it into Wald in Pinzgau.

18 ☐ Turn left in the village square along the Trattenbach and walk as far as an old watermill.

19 ☐ Bear right away from the mill, through forest to Seerain.

20 ☐ Turn left then right at the farm buildings of Seerain.

21 ☐ Follow an access lane, past another old mill to rejoin the road to Neukirchen above the old castle of Hohenneukirchen.

If time allows, a visit to the old castle could round off a memorable day.

F • THE TAUERNKREUZ PASS

9 miles (14km). 6–7 hours. Moderate/Strenuous.
4,175ft (1,272m) ascent.

As this walk finishes on the far side of the Tauern mountain range, it will be necessary either to check the times of the post bus service between Mittersill and the Tauern valley and to plan the timing of the walk accordingly, or make arrangements to be met by a car at the end of the walk.

There is quite a lot of climbing involved in following this route, but there is the advantage of having an admirably sited mountain hut on top of the Tauernkreuz Pass, at the end of the climb. From the hut, those with enough energy to spare, can climb the distinctive peak of the Tauernkogel — 9,810ft (2,989m). From the summit it will be possible to enjoy views of the nearby Grossvenediger peak — 12,058ft (3,674m) and its attendant glaciers.

The route starts in the Amertal above Mittersill and climbs steadily along an easy track before rising steeply beneath the Grosser Schrankeck peak. The path then keeps to an easier angle, south across the Tauernbach valley, before its last rise towards the welcome sight of the St Pöltener hut on the Tauernkreuz Pass — 8,143ft (2,481m). The descent, though steep in places is straightforward and follows the southern Tauernbach into the Tauern valley, reaching the valley road near a convenient bus stop.

The Route

1 ☐ Leave the Amertal road south of Mittersill at the bus stop on the hairpin bend below Schösswend.

2 ☐ Follow the access road along the Felberbach valley. **Note**: the valley is not named on some maps.

3 ☐ Walk through quiet meadows following the river upstream past the Schösswend Tauernhaus and later the Tauernhaus-Spital mountain hut.

4 ☐ Climb by a series of bends towards the Hintersee.

This lake, slightly off the route, makes an interesting diversion before starting on the steepest part of the pass.

5 ☐   A little to the north of the lake, a path on the left crosses the river. Follow this, past a small hut and into the forest.

6 ☐   Climb by a zigzag route steeply uphill, crossing a side stream many times.

Look out for the cool waters of the Weinbrunn spring about 400ft (122m) above the small hut.

7 ☐   Leave the forest and cross a small alp with the single building of Schonau Alm farmstead.

8 ☐   Turn right across the hillside then slant left, uphill on an easier slope.

9 ☐   Begin to follow the contours, then cross the side valley of the Tauernbach.

10 ☐   At a footpath junction marked by a calvary shrine, bear left and uphill. Go past a lake, known as the Plattsee.

11 ☐   Climb through a boulder field and aim for the St Pöltener hut which marks the col of the Tauernkreuz Pass.

The hut makes a welcome stop. If time allows, the climb of the Tauernkogel — 9,810ft (2,989m), which is to the west of the col, is highly recommended.

12 ☐   Walk ahead, downhill at first through a boulder field, then later alongside the south Tauernbach.

There are some good views of the southern peaks of the Venediger group on the way down from the pass.

13 ☐   Bear right at a footpath junction. Do not cross the stream.

14 ☐   At a path junction marked by a shrine, walk ahead, then zigzag steeply downhill and eventually into pine forest.

15 ☐   Turn left at the valley road and walk as far as Matrier Tauernhaus restaurant where there is also a bus stop for the journey back.

G • GEISSTEIN

9 miles (14km). 8–9 hours. Strenuous.
5,130ft (1,563m) ascent.

Although this is a steep and long climb it is one which should be well within the capabilities of any fit hillwalker. Starting in Stuhlfelden village, the route is easy to follow. At first it is simply along the service track to the Bürgl hut and beneath the south face of the Geisstein. Steep paths which involve a little easy scrambling lead directly to the summit. For the descent, a south-westerly path is followed into the Sintersbach Scharte where there is, if necessary, an escape route to the Bürgl hut. The final part of the route is to the south from the col, then steeply downhill into Mittersill.

This walk is only suitable for hard walkers and those with a good head for heights. Boots are essential and remember that as there is a considerable height difference between Stuhlfelden and the summit, the weather could deteriorate on top, so take protective clothing and a spare sweater in your rucksack.

The Route

1 □   The walk starts from Stuhlfelden village which is served by both rail and post bus. If travelling by car, park where it will not interfere with other road users. Mittersill is only a couple of bus stops away so there should be no problems collecting the car at the end of the walk.

If time allows have a look round Stuhlfelden's baroque church and its tranquil graveyard.

2 □   Follow the side road due north from the church and into the forested Stuhlfelden Bach valley.

3 □   Follow the winding road out of the valley, through forest and meadowland uphill across the farming area of Bam.

4 □   After the last farm building and a calvary shrine, the surface of the road deteriorates into a rough track as it climbs the forested hillside.

The cool shade of the forest will make the steep climb comparatively easy.

5 ☐   Drop down to the Muhltal arm of the upper Stuhlfelden valley. Turn left and cross over to follow the north bank upstream.

6 ☐   The forest slowly thins out into scrubby alpine growth. Cross the more open hillside and reach the Bürgl hut.

The hut will be a welcome break, but resist the temptation to linger.

7 ☐   Climb from the hut to a fork in the path and bear right.

8 ☐   Turn left at a footpath junction and zigzag uphill on increasingly rocky ground.

Spare time to admire the alpine flowers on this south-facing hillside.

9 ☐   Take care on the final rocky section leading to the summit of the Geisstein — 7,755ft (2,363m).

The view from the top makes the climb worthwhile. Use the map to pinpoint all the surrounding peaks.

10 ☐   Bear right, downhill, away from the summit along a broad ridge and down to the Sintersbach Scharte.

If the climb has proved tiring for any members of the party, a left turn downhill, will quickly take them back to the Bürgl hut and if necessary, a night's accommodation or even transport back to Stuhlfelden.

11 ☐   Walk half-right over rocky ground uphill away from the col and cross a wide combe.

12 ☐   Cross the shallow col of Rosswegscharte and go downhill on the rock-strewn hillside.

13 ☐   Bear left at a footpath junction by a stream, the Burkbach.

14 ☐   Follow the zigzag path into forest and continue downhill to the open pastures opposite Brand.

15 ☐   Follow the east (left) bank of the stream.

16 ☐   Join an access track and follow it to the main road.

17 ☐   Turn left and walk into Mittersill.

The bus stop is conveniently near the junction of the final track with the main road.

H • THE HABACHTAL

18 miles (29km). 8–9 hours. Moderate.
4,539ft (1,383m) ascent.

One of the problems involved in walking along alpine valleys, is they tend to end in high mountains impenetrable to all except skilled mountaineers. The Habachtal is typical, but like others of this nature, it does show the awe-inspiring beauty of the mountains and glaciers close at hand.

Starting easily enough by crossing the riverside meadows below Neukirchen, the route enters Habachtal near the hamlet of Haus. An access track, closed to all except local traffic, follows the Habach stream through mature forest and across clearings made centuries ago by the ancestors of today's hill farmers. The track effectively ends at the Alpenrose hut and from there a mountain path climbs steadily towards the valley's headwaters. From the highest point of the path, the Habachkees (glacier) reaches down into the valley from the rocky spires of northern and north eastern ridges leading off the Plattiger-Habach peak. A short traverse leads to the Neue Thüringer hut and a zigzag path leads back towards the valley. The return is by the same route used for the ascent, but the views being in the opposite direction, are quite different to those earlier in the day.

The Route

1 □ Walk down to and across the railway line next to Neukirchen station. Follow the road as far as the river.

2 □ Turn left, downstream across meadowland as far as the hamlet of Haus.

3 □ Turn right on the valley road and climb alongside the Habach , passing in and out of mature pine forest.

Look out for an old watermill, on the right about a quarter of a mile (0.4km) beyond Haus.

4 □ Follow the road for about 5 miles (8km) to the Alpenrose hut which makes a good coffee stop.

5 □ Continue uphill on what soon becomes a mountain path along the narrowing upper valley.

131

6 ☐ Ignoring a side path on the left continue to follow the river upstream, crossing side streams as necessary.

7 ☐ Cross the river to the right, then swing round, to the left uphill through the rocky debris of the combe.

Look up at the crevassed face of the Habachkees (kees is the local dialect word for glacier) and the soaring ridges on either side of the Plattinger-Habach peak — 10,548ft (3,214m).

8 ☐ Keep left at a path junction to follow a more level route, across two mountain streams to the Neue Thüringer hut — 7,352ft (2,240m).

Rest and enjoy the atmosphere of the hut before beginning the descent. If necessary food and accommodation for the night can be found here.

9 ☐ Follow the slanting path downhill away from the hut.

10 ☐ Cross a stream and begin to zigzag down the steep hillside.

Try to resist the temptation to cut corners on the descent. If you go directly downhill it is more tiring and could easily lead to an injury following a slip; also direct or 'unofficial' paths cause erosion.

11 ☐ Join the main path in the valley bottom and turn right.

Look out for a waterfall high on the right a little beyond the path junction.

12 ☐ Follow the valley path and road all the way back via Haus, pausing for rest and refreshment at as many of the welcoming *Gasthöfe* and restaurants as time and finances allow.

7 KITZBÜHEL

Map

Kompass Wanderkarte (1:50,000 series) Sheet 29; Kitzbüheler Alpen.

How to Get There

Road

1 • South-east across Europe by motorway via Munich to Kufstein, then east via St Johann in Tirol to Kitzbühel.

2 • South to Basel, east to Zurich and Lake Constance (Bodensee). Enter Austria at Dornbirn and join the Inn valley via the Arlberg Pass. Leave the Inn valley *Autobahn* at the Wörgl interchange. Go east via Brixen to Kitzbühel.

Rail

Trans-European, Arlberg Express to Innsbruck. Local service to Kitzbühel.

Air

Nearest airports at Salzburg and Innsbruck. Rail or bus connections.

The Area

Kitzbühel is probably best known as a ski resort and less so as a summer walking area, but what is least known is its history. Copper deposits first attracted people to settle in this district in the Bronze Age. As early as the ninth century BC, it had developed as an important trading centre.

It was, however, during the fifteenth century AD that serious copper mining took place: two notable mines, the Fugger and Rosenberger were sunk close by to work the ore, and later silver was discovered. The original miners' settlement just off the town centre is still recognisable from its preserved houses including that of the Mining Magistrate who looked after the legal aspect of claims and other mining rights. The town granary houses a fascinating museum of a time when Kitzbühel was an important mining centre.

The name Kitzbühel comes from the original ruling family, the Chizzos. The first recorded mention of the name of the town, is in documents dating from 1165 when it was called 'Chizbuhel'. The

Kitzbühel with the Kitzbüheler Horn in the background

Chizzos held sway over the district, controlling its mining riches and living in a castle, the site of which is now the Heimatmuseum, or folk museum.

Mud from the nearby Schwarzsee was considered to have health-giving properties and Kitzbühel developed as a spa during the nineteenth century. It was however the excellent snow which attracted winter sports enthusiasts to the town and it became a leading ski resort before World War I.

Walking is comparatively easy by alpine standards, none of the local hills are steep or rocky to any great extent and the broad pine-clad ridges offer an extensive number of excursions. It is practical to extend most of the walks described in this section of the guide, or to plan an almost unlimited number of longer routes. Even though the mountains around Kitzbühel are gentle, the giants of the Hohe Tauern are not far away to the south. This National Park area has Austria's highest mountains, the Grossglockner and the Grossvenediger, which make a vast panorama of snow and ice when viewed from many of the high-level walks above Kitzbühel. The Wilder Kaiser range is much closer, to the north of the town, and often appears like a sheer wall of pale yellow limestone above St Johann, the next town beyond Kitzbühel.

As expected in an area devoted to winter sports, the hills are liberally served by cable cars and chairlifts. Not all are open in summer, but most are, and offer easy access onto hillsides and summits.

Activities other than hillwalking range from hang gliding, horse riding, golf, tennis (indoor as well as open-air), swimming, boating, flower and animal festivals and guided walks.

From the end of May to mid-October, anyone staying in Kitzbühel can take part in organised walks led by qualified guides. The programme is free and the walks are very much of an easy nature, usually calling on some feature in the area, perhaps a mountain hut, or a local farmer who will demonstrate his skill at making cheese. Check with the tourist office for details of this scheme. Badges, a popular feature of mountain walking in Austria, are awarded to participants who manage more than three tours.

Useful Information

Local Tourist Office
Fremdenverkehrsverband
A-6370 Kitzbühel
☎ 05356-2155 and 2272

Accommodation
From very high class hotels to *Gasthöfe* and rented rooms. Camp site by the shores of the Schwarzsee.

Cable Cars and Chairlifts
Cable Cars Hahnenkammbahn, Hornbahn, Hornköpfl.
Chairlifts Birchlalmbahn, Streifalm, Klausen.

Recommended Excursions
Kitzbühler Horn Alpine Garden Alpine plants in their natural setting.
Aurach Wildpark European mountain animals.
Salzburg Historic city, with imposing fortress. Mozart museum and festival with concerts. Hellbrunn Palace and its water features.
Innsbruck Famous town on the river Inn.Museums, shops, restaurants. Excursions into the Karwendel mountains.
Grossglockner Road High-level motor road (toll) south from Zell am See.

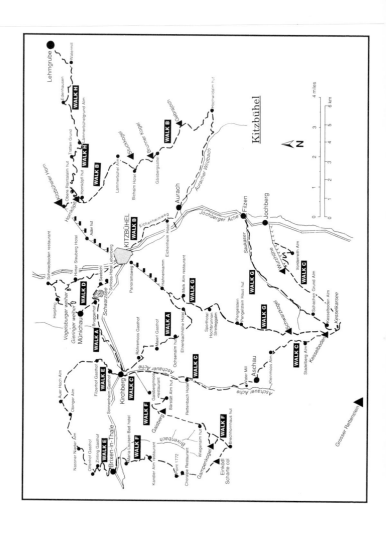

Kitzbühel

A • THE HAHNENKAMM

7 miles (11km). 3–4 hours. Easy.
3,410ft (1,039m) descent.

The Hahnenkamm is one of the most famous European skiing areas. Large sections of mountainside have been carefully cleared of natural pine forest, opening up the mountain to walkers as well as skiers. Another benefit of this clearance is the wide-ranging views of the higher and more dramatic peaks to the north and south.

By using the Hahnenkammbahn cable car to reach the summit from Kitzbühel, most of the initial effort is removed and so the walk is an ideal first day's excursion into the local mountains. Downhill paths and trackways follow north-facing slopes, crossing meadows and ski slopes, but also in and out of forest to escape the sun on hot days. Kirchberg marks the final descent and then a valley walk leads to the Schwarzsee, Kitzbühel's lido. From here it is an easy stroll through the forest to Kitzbühel.

The Route

1 ☐   Take the cable car from its lower station next to Kitzbühel railway station to the summit of the Hahnenkamm — 5,432ft (1,655m).

The building to the right of the upper station is one of a series of meteorological units collating weather data throughout the Alps.

2 ☐   Follow the road to the Ehrenbachhöhe Hotel. Climb the short distance to the top of Ehrenbachhöhe — 5,914ft (1,802m).

3 ☐   Return to the hotel and turn right, away from the road along a path passing in and out of patches of woodland as it descends the hillside.

4 ☐   Swing right and make for the Ochsenalm hut.

5 ☐   Continue downhill to the Maierl *Gasthof* and cross its access road.

6 ☐   Walk down the open hillside towards the Bradseiten valley.

7 ☐   Do not cross the valley, but swing left, to follow the path through a clearing and join a mountain road above the Röhremoos *Gasthof*.

8 ☐   Turn right along the road and walk down to Kirchberg.

Walking on the Hahnenkamm, with a view of the Kitzbüheler Horn

Kirchberg is an interesting little village, not quite so cosmopolitan as Kitzbühel, but most accommodating for those seeking refreshment.

9 ☐   Walk to the right through the village as far as the river. Do not cross, but follow a path along its southern bank.

10 ☐   Cross the river and railway line by following the side road from Klausen and walk towards the stream, the Aschauer Ache.

11 ☐   Take the first path on the right beyond the railway.

12 ☐   Walk alongside the track as far as Schwarzsee.

13 ☐   Go round the lake to the left.

Swimming and boating are popular in and on the Schwarzsee so take a swimming costume if you want a bathe at the end of the walk.

14 ☐   There is a choice of routes back to Kitzbühel from the lake. Take whichever seems the most attractive at the time.

B • KITZBÜHELER HORN

12 miles (19km). 6–7 hours. Moderate.
4,053ft (1,235m) descent.

Here is a pleasant high-level ramble which keeps its height, gained by mechanical means, from the summit of the mountain for almost half of the walk. The path follows hillside contours and is mostly above the tree line until it reaches the Auracher valley. Turning right at the Hochwildes hut the descent is easy and at Aurach in the valley bottom, a path through local meadows leads directly to the southern outskirts of Kitzbühel.

A short diversion at the beginning of the walk will take in the alpine garden, just below the summit of Kitzbüheler Horn, and an alpine zoo in the Auracher valley is added interest near the end.

The Route

1 □   Take the cable car by way of Pletzer Alm to the top of the Kitzbüheler Horn — 6,551ft (1,996m).

The panoramic view from the summit is the finest in the district and takes in the Wilder Kaiser range to the north and the giants of the Hohe Tauern to the south. The Grossglockner — 12,462ft (3,797m) and the Grossvenediger — 12,058ft (3,674m) should be easy to identify as well as many of the other high points of this range.

2 □   Walk down the track to the alpine garden (*Alpen-Blumengarten*).

Many of the flowers of the Alps and mountain ranges further afield are displayed in this natural setting. Some are quite rare and difficult to propagate.

3 □   Follow the access track as far as Alpenhaus Kitzbüheler Horn.

4 □   Turn left on a well defined path and go down the open hillside.

5 □   Join an access road and turn left. Climb to the mountain settlement of Lammerbühel Alm.

6 □   Cross a broad col and go steeply down to the Bichalm Hotel.

7 □   Turn left away from the hotel and follow the contours of the hillside beneath the rocky summits of Stuckkogel and Brunner Kogel.

8 □   Go past the upper station of a chairlift towards the lonely

farmhouse at Gäisbergsattel.

9 ☐   Keep right at a path junction, continuing to follow easy contours above the tree line.

10 ☐   Bear right at a path junction on the col of Gebrajoch. Cross the next side valley.

11 ☐   Work your way round the west slope of Gebra, passing through sections of forest and open hillside.

12 ☐   Drop down to the Hochwildalm hut and turn right, down its access track.

13 ☐   Follow the track downhill alongside a stream, the Auracher Wildbach.

About half way down the valley, a signposted side road leads to the Wildpark, an alpine zoo.

14 ☐   Follow the road into Aurach.

15 ☐   Do not go as far as the main road, but turn right through the village. Cross a side stream and walk as far as the Eichenheim Hotel.

16 ☐   Follow the path, to the left of the hotel, through meadows and below the edge of the forest, as far as Stockerdörfl on the outskirts of Kitzbühel. The path is called the Eichenheimweg.

C • WURZHÖHE

13 miles (21km). 6–7 hours. Moderate.

A short climb from the Jochberg chairlift quickly reaches the summit of Wurzhöhe — 5,707ft (1,739m). From this point a long open ridge dotted with clumps of scrub pine, leads in an easy line to the south-west where a broad col with a tiny lake marks the turning point. Easy paths to the north work their way into the Aschauer valley where gentle road walking and a riverside path lead to Kirchberg.

The Route

1 ☐   Take the valley bus south to Jochberg and then use the chairlift to reach the lower slopes of the Wurzhöhe.

2 ☐   Bear left away from the chairlift, diagonally uphill to the farm-stead at Vorderreith Alm.

3 ☐   Swing right and zigzag uphill past the higher farmstead at Wurzalm. Ignore the access track on the right.

4 ☐   Climb the final slope to the top of the Wurzhöhe.

Pause to admire the view and look ahead to the south-west along the broad crest of the ridge.

5 ☐   Turn left from the summit and follow the ridge, going through narrow bands of scrub and mature pines, but mainly on open ground.

The ridge top is well covered with alpine flowers. The red alpenrose flourishes quite well. Marmots and mountain birds use its sunny crest.

6 ☐   Walk along the ridge, over the summit of Talsenhöhe — 6,326ft (1,928m).

7 ☐   Go down into the wide col and turn right past the tiny lake known locally as the Blau Lacke (Blue Lake), but marked on most maps as Kesselkarsee.

8 ☐   Walk across the open hillside to the second footpath junction and then ahead, downhill to a group of farmsteads on Stadelberg Alm.

9 ☐   Follow the access road north, above the tree line to a second group of farms at Kleinmoos Alm.

10 ☐   Turn left, downhill through sections of forest. Cross an access track and follow the forest edge into the village of Aschau.

Aschau is the first convenient refreshment stop on the walk.

11 ☐   Walk along the valley road.

An old watermill on the outskirts of Aschau is just one of many fine old buildings in this valley.

12 ☐   Move away from the river, still following the road, and a little way beyond the Rettenbach Hotel cross a side stream.

13 ☐   Take the forest path on the left, cross the river to follow its western or true left bank.

14 ☐   Walk through forest and then open meadows and join the road into Kirchberg.

15 ☐   Take the bus back from Kirchberg.

D • SCHWARZSEE

5$\frac{1}{2}$ miles (9km). 2–3 hours. Easy.

This forest and lakeside walk is dual-purpose, suitable for either rainy days which prevent any high-level expeditions, or days when the power of the sun again makes one feel lazy. The shade offered by pine trees competes with the cool waters of the three lakes visited *en route*. Swimming takes place in all of them.

The route follows a series of interlinked paths and forest tracks, gently up and downhill across the Wandergebiet Bichlach, Kitzbühel's local rambling woodlands. Although the walk is described only as far as the Schmiedboden restaurant, it can be extended for several miles towards Oberndorf by using the continuing footpaths. Woodland paths can be a little confusing, but most are clearly signposted. Always look out for the sign to your next feature along the way.

The Route

1 □   Walk out of Kitzbühel by way of the road past the Schloss-hotel Lebenberg.

2 □   Follow the road to the south of the low hill of Lebenberg, as far as the Seebichl restaurant.

3 □   Walk on towards the Schwarzsee. Follow its shoreline towards the Bruggerhof and the camp site.

4 □   Use the woodland path to reach the hamlet of Münichau.

5 □   Turn right along the side road towards the Gieringer Weiher lake.

6 □   Continue along the road, through open meadowland and past occasional houses. Bear right at the road junction at Hörpfing.

7 □   Walk onwards as far as the Schmiedboden restaurant for an early lunch stop.

8 □   Retrace the route back to the road junction at Rain.

9 □   Turn left and walk along a track as far as a 'T' junction.

10 □   Go right on a wide path, through forest and down to the Vogelsburger Weiher lake.

11 ☐ Left, uphill from the lake to Hinter Steurberg Hotel.

12 ☐ Ahead, downhill by path from the hotel and left at a path junction. Walk through a stretch of forest and out into meadowland.

13 ☐ Right at a path junction and towards a group of houses at Achrain.

14 ☐ Do not use the access road, but go left uphill and into the forest surrounding Lebenberg.

15 ☐ Walk on and downhill to the left of Schloss-hotel Lebenberg.

E • RAUHER KOGEL

7 miles (11km). 4–5 hours. Moderate.
2,462ft (750m) ascent.

No cable cars or chairlifts climb the forested slopes of Rauher Kogel — 5,186ft (1,580m) and as a result, the hillsides to the north of the village of Kirchberg are less popular than those with easier access. This does not infer that the Rauher Kogel is inferior to its better favoured neighbours. Gentle slopes and shaded forest tracks lead quietly into attractive clearings, where the land has been farmed for generations by descendants of the men who hacked land from the original forest.

From Kirchberg easy tracks climb from the south-east, through forest and across Rauher Kogel. Beyond the hilltop, clearings appear on sunny slopes and the path wanders on, taking the easiest gradient until it reaches a group of high-level *Gasthöfe*. These south-facing hostelries mark the end of the mountain section of the walk, and from there the way is downhill into Brixen.

As the restaurant facilities come near the end of the walk, it might be advisable to carry a packed lunch rather than rely on reaching a *Gasthof* in time for a midday meal.

The Route

1 ☐ Take the Wörgl route bus or train as far as Kirchberg.

2 ☐ Walk into the village square and cross the river, using the side road to the Sonnenheim *Gasthof.*

3 ☐ Take the left fork at the *Gasthof* and walk uphill through a

narrow stretch of forest, then across a meadow.

4 ☐ Pass a couple of houses and go through another section of pine forest and join a road.

5 ☐ Turn right along the road, then left and right as far as the Filzerhof *Gasthof.*

6 ☐ Uphill from the Filzerhof, where a track enters dense pine forest and climbs the eastern spur of Rauher Kogel to its summit.

7 ☐ Cross the summit and walk along the wide tree-covered ridge to a path junction.

8 ☐ Go right at the junction, then right again in about 200yd (183m).

9 ☐ Follow the path out of the forest and across a clearing grazed by alpine cattle. Turn left at the farmhouse at Auer Hoch Alm.

10 ☐ Walk back into the forest and turn left onto another path.

11 ☐ Right at a fork and into the centre of a clearing marked by a small building.

12 ☐ Turn right on a narrow path away from the clearing and walk through more forest to another clearing and the farmhouse of Obinger Alm.

13 ☐ Continue ahead again into forest and on to Nasser Nieder Alm.

14 ☐ Cross a footpath junction and skirt the forest edge at the top boundary of a triangular-shaped clearing.

15 ☐ Join the forest road at a group of buildings and follow it round to a road junction and the Offenhof *Gasthof.*

The Offenhof and other nearby Gasthöfe *are the only chance of buying refreshments on this walk, and may be used for a late lunch.*

16 ☐ Turn left at the road junction and walk downhill as far as the second bend below the Zinting *Gasthof.*

17 ☐ Turn left steeply downhill by the field path leading directly towards the village square of Brixen-in-Thale, where convenient buses or trains run back to Kitzbühel.

The church and unspoilt old houses around the square are a major feature of Brixen.

F • GAISBERG

9 miles (14km). 4–5 hours. Moderate.

An easy ridge stretches south-west from the summit of Gaisberg — 5,799ft (1,767m). The mountain is an easy climb, most of the height being gained by the chairlift from Kirchberg.

The ridge is mostly grass-covered and well above the upper limits of the forest, however, odd outcrops of rock make the route more interesting.

Conveniently spaced huts will make the journey all the more enjoyable; the day can be spent walking from hut to hut above the tree line as far as the last downhill stretch to Brixen, which will then be mainly in forest.

The Route

1 □   Travel either by bus or train to reach Kirchberg.

2 □   Walk along the Sperten Tal road, south from the village square, as far as the river bridge.

3 □   Take the chairlift to the Gaisbergmoos restaurant.

4 □   Walk to the left slightly uphill from the upper station and restaurant, following the upper limits of a pine wood as far as the Bärstätt Alm hut.

5 □   Turn right, taking the second path uphill.

6 □   Climb in one big sweep to the summit of Gaisberg.

The best view is to the south, encompassing the Hohe Tauern range. Closer to hand but still south and in the middle distance is the rocky Grosser Rettenstein — 7,752ft (2,362m) at the head of the Sperten Tal. This is the highest peak in the immediate locality of Kitzbühel.

7 □   Follow the part-grass, part-rocky ridge, down to a broad col marked by the Wiegenalm hut, an ideal place to stop for coffee.

Gaisberg's south ridge is often covered with the red flowers of alpenrose, a plant related to the rhododendron.

8 □   Walk on from the Wiegenalm hut uphill — then down to the Brechhornhaus hut on the col at Kreuz Joch.

An optional diversion before reaching Kreuz Joch would be to climb the Gampenkogel — 6,420ft (1,956m).

9 ☐   Turn right, downhill on a wide track which skirts the top of a small pine wood.

10 ☐   Fork right and climb up to the Einködl Scharte.

11 ☐   Downhill to a junction of four tracks. Bear half right, away and downhill to Restaurant Choralpe, close to the top station of a chairlift. Walk on towards a small shrine at point 1772.

12 ☐   Turn sharply to the right and follow an access track downhill. Follow the upper edge of dense pine forest.

13 ☐   Enter the pine forest and walk down a broadening ridge.

14 ☐   Pass a forest cabin and out to a clearing and the Kandler Alm restaurant.

15 ☐   Follow the access track downhill until it passes beneath a supply cable.

16 ☐   Turn right and follow the field path down to the road end at the Maria-Louisen-Bad hotel.

17 ☐   Walk down the road, past a camp site and into Brixen for the bus back to Kitzbühel.

A cable-car station above Kitzbühel

146

G • SCHWARZKOGEL

11¹/₂ miles (19km). 5–6 hours. Moderate.

This is another ridge walk where the height, gained easily, is held almost until the end of the walk. The ridge is above the tree line and apart from a few isolated pockets, trees are not encountered until the last downhill stretch. This is in the Saukaser valley, where the path and forest track follow a river draining the north-east face of the ridge all the way to Filzen.

From the top of the Hahnenkamm, the path wanders easily more or less south all the time, past a series of hotels and restaurants until it reaches the col with the Kesselkarsee in its centre. A left turn leads down to the Saukaser valley.

The Route

1 ☐   Use the Hahnenkammbahn to reach the Bergstation hotel.

2 ☐   Follow the footpath known as the Panoramaweg along the crest of the ridge to the Melk Alm restaurant (only open in the winter) where four tracks meet.

3 ☐   Take the furthest right path passing beneath two ski-lifts to reach another path and track complex.

4 ☐   Go left down to the Sporthotel Hochbrunnon at Streiteggalm (again only open in the winter).

Most of the hotels and restaurants are only open in winter, so do not rely upon finding any open on the early part of the walk. The Pengelstein Haus slightly further along the ridge, should be open in summer.

5 ☐   Follow the path back onto the ridge and swing right. Ignore paths to the left.

6 ☐   Walk beneath its service cable to the Pengelstein Haus hut.

7 ☐   Go along the wide ridge, rocky in places, but mostly covered by light vegetation.

8 ☐   Climb the Schwarzkogel — 6,662ft (2,030m).

Pause to admire the view before walking down Schwarzkogel's shaly

147

south slope.

9 □   Continue south along the ridge, over the minor summit of Kesselboden — 6,098ft (1,858m) and then down to the col and the Kesselkarsee.

10 □   Do not walk beyond the lake, but go sharp left, downhill to a group of farm buildings at Kesselboden Alm.

11 □   Follow the path downhill and enter the forest at Schachen Grund Alm.

12 □   Join the Saukaser river and follow it, swopping sides as dictated by the route.

13 □   Join a forest track and continue downstream enjoying the shade of the pine forest.

14 □   Walk to Filzen and either catch the bus or follow side roads parallel to the main road back to Kitzbühel.

H • TRATTEN GRUND

8 miles (13km). 4 hours. Moderate.
4,073ft (1,241m) descent.

For the last walk in this section return to the Kitzbüheler Horn and then follow a meandering route, roughly eastwards, into the Pillersee valley. The path quickly leaves behind all contact with the paraphernalia of winter sports and the only signs of man's handiwork are the mountain farms or alms, standing amidst clearings on the forested hillside.

The walk is easy to follow and has no steep gradients after the initial descent from the Kitzbüheler Horn summit. Forest and alpine pastures lead gradually downhill to Weissach where local tracks lead on to the finish at Lehmgrube in the Pillersee valley.

The Route

1 □   Climb to the top of the Kitzbüheler Horn — 6,651ft (1,996m) by the cable car.

2 ☐   Walk downhill to the Hornköpfl hut.

3 ☐   Turn left and climb across the summit of the Hornköpfl — 3,877ft (1,772m). Go down on the other side, following an access track to the Obere Raintalalm hut.

4 ☐   Zigzag downhill beneath a ski-lift to a path and track junction at Unterraintalalm.

5 ☐   Go left, then almost immediately right at a fork to reach the group of farmsteads at Tratten Grund.

6 ☐   Bear right, away from the farm access road, downhill and across the Trattenbach river.

7 ☐   Climb through forest to Lämmerbühelgrund Alm.

8 ☐   Follow the contours round the hillside and then go downhill, in and out of forest to the small settlement of Edenhausen.

9 ☐   Turn right along the access track and follow it across the open hillside of Weissach.

10 ☐   Above the Pletzer-Graben valley swing round above a complex of minor roads and into Lehmgrube.

The small watermill at the beginning of the side road complex is used to make wood pulp.

11 ☐   Catch the bus or train back to Kitzbühel via St Johann in Tirol.

Edelweiss

8 KALS

Map

Kompass Wanderkarte (1:50,000 series) Sheet 48; Kals am Grossglockner.

How to Get There

Road

1 • Direct Route East on the German *Autobahn* system via Munich to Kufstein (road numbers 8 (E11) and 93 (E86), then south through St Johann and Kitzbühel to Mittersill. South again on road 108 via the Felber Tauern Tunnel to Peischlach; Kals is about 8 miles (13km), to the north-east at the head of a side road.

2 • As above to Munich, then south on the E6 to Innsbruck. North-east along the A12 to Wörgl. East to Kitzbühel and south-south-east to Mittersill, then south as above.

3 • Continue on the *Autobahn* to Salzburg, then south to Bischofshofen. South-west and west to Mittersill, then follow route **1**.

Rail

Main line Trans-European service via Innsbruck to Zell am See. Post bus via Mittersill and Peischlach.

Air

Via Salzburg or Innsbruck, then rail to Zell am See and bus as above.

The Area

Nestling in a sunny valley beneath the south face of the Grossglockner peak, Kals is probably better known among mountaineers who come down to its comfort after spending days, or even weeks, scrambling amongst the rocky ridges and crossing the crevassed glaciers. The Grossglockner — 12,465ft (3,798m), while being the highest peak in the group and also in Austria, is not the central point of this complex mass of rock and ice. This honour is reserved for the Eiskögle — 11,270ft (3,434m), and from it a whole complex of glacier-lined ridges radiate, splitting into yet further sub ranges.

Kals need not be a base purely for the serious mountaineer. It makes an ideal centre to explore the side valleys and high-level paths which cross the slopes beneath the Glockner giants. Surrounded by protected areas of special interest, Kals is within the boundaries of the Austrian National Park. Here is a small village relatively undeveloped by the rash of hotels, cable cars and car parks, which often mark the passing of a once attractive and unspoilt area. The National Park status ensures that Kals remains a place to visit for a tranquil holiday amongst dramatic mountain scenery.

Walking can be as varied as ability and inclination allow. It can range from simple valley wandering, to following easy contour-hugging paths across hillsides with far ranging views, or along well marked tracks to friendly mountain huts offering simple, but sustaining refreshment. More ambitious routes can be used to reach the lower peaks below the majestic snow-covered summits of the Glockner group.

People have lived in the valleys around Kals for many generations and their simple part-timbered hill farmhouses would be still recognisable to the great-grandparents of the present owners. The church with its slender spire is the focal point of village life. Water mills, some still used to grind locally grown corn, use the power of the Kaiserbach and make interesting diversions on several of the valley walks.

There is only one chairlift, the Glocknerblick, which is used to gain height when exploring the western side of the Kalser valley. Paths to the east have all been well designed and help the walker to climb hillsides with the minimum of effort.

Useful Information

Tourist Office
Fremdenverkehrsverband
Kals am Grossglockner
Osttirol
A 9981
☎ 04876-211

Accommodation
Ranges from family-run three star hotels to guest houses and rented accommodation. Nearest camp site is at Matrei-in-Osttirol.

Chairlifts
From Kals The Glocknerblick climbs from Grossdorf on the western side of Kals village to a restaurant at its upper station.

The Pasterzen glacier from the Franz-Joseph Haus

From Matrei in Osttirol Two-stage chairlift from Klaunz to the Goldried restaurant.

Glacier Viewing

For the best views of the Glockner range and its glaciers, climb the Blauspitze — 8,333ft (2,539m) above the Glocknerblick chairlift, or from the summit of the Schönleisten Spitze — 9,222ft (2,810m) to the south-east of Kals.

It is possible to reach the foot of the main glacier, the Mittleres Pasterzenkees, from the Franz-Joseph Haus hotel at the end of the side road from the bottom of the Grossglockner road. Road access is via either Lienz and Heiligenblut, or via Zell am See, but it is possible to walk to the Franz-Joseph Haus from Kals (see the Franz-Joseph Hohe walk) and stay overnight, returning by an alternative route the next day.

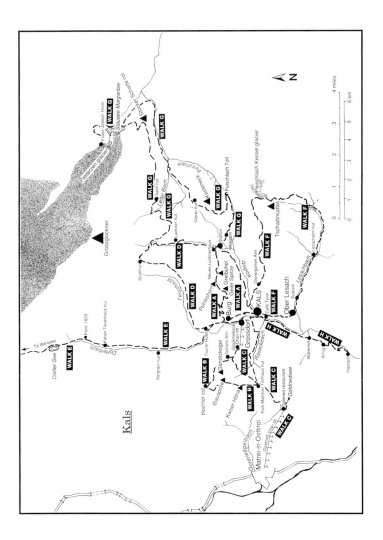

Kals

WALK A · WALK B · WALK C · WALK D · WALK E · WALK F · WALK G · WALK H

Grossglockner
Franz-Joseph Hotel
Stausee Margaritze
Pasterzen Glacier
Leiter Bach
Salm hut
Glorer hut
Kastner bach
Peischlach
Peischlach Törl
Peischlach Kessel glacier
Peischlach Kessel glacier
Tschadinsattel
Lesachalm hut
Lesachbach
Stadlhut
Teischnitz
Studlhut
Neues Lucknerhaus
Lucknerhut
Glatschacher Station
Wrigel
Ködnitz
Glorergarten Alm
Ober Lesach
Ruissio
Pohlsebon
Gradbühl
Glate Spitze
Burg
Grossdorf
KALS
Cafe Tyrol
Gasse-Glacier
Lucknerhut
Watermill
Arnig
Haslach
Rasseckbach
Ganotz Alm
Bergbraun hut
Tauner Hotel
Hochtor col
Blauspitze
Ganotzkogel
Kaiser Höhne
Kals Matreier Törlhaus hut
Goldried restaurant
Goldriedsee
Goldriedbahn
Matrei-in-Osttirol
Geiseit
Dorfer See
To Weissee
Point 1825
Kalser Tauernhaus hut
Dörferbach

Grossglockner

N

0 1 2 3 4 miles
0 1 2 3 4 5 6 km

A • THE KÖDNITZ VALLEY AND THE POHLESHORN

7^1/$_2$ miles (12km). 4–5 hours. Moderate/Strenuous.
3,069ft (935m) ascent.

Although this walk involves some climbing, it is still an ideal introduction to Kals. It takes in the village with its twin valleys and climbs an attractively situated hilltop to give a bird's eye view of the area. The well placed Neues Lucknerhaus hut, about halfway around the walk, can be used for lunch and will give an interesting introduction to alpine huts to anyone visiting the high mountains for the first time.

The route starts by the village church in Kals and follows an easy track above the Ködnitz stream before climbing to the Neues Lucknerhaus. A gently rising path then crosses the hillside below the Fiegerhorn to reach the highest point of the walk on the summit of the Pohleshorn. The path descends gradually into forest and then follows a steepening course into the Kalserbach valley. Crossing the valley road, the walk follows a stream, the Kalserbach, through Grossdorf where a short road walk leads back to the centre of Kals.

The Route

1 ☐ From Kals church follow the side lane north-eastwards above the Ködnitz river.

Ancient watermills line the river bank, using the free power of a stream which flows directly from the south-facing Ködnitz glacier beneath the summit of the Grossglockner.

2 ☐ Continue through meadowland as far as an access road into the wooded upper valley.

3 ☐ Turn right along the roughly surfaced road and climb to the left, around a hairpin bend and past the bottom station of a supply cable serving the Glorer hut. Walk as far as the Neues Lucknerhaus hut and restaurant.

The tree-shaded Neues Lucknerhaus — 6,511ft (1,984m), will make an ideal lunch stop.

4 ☐ Follow the signposted path to the west of the Neues Lucknerhaus. Climb through the pine forest and out onto the open Greiwiesen hillside.

Greiwiesen is covered by alpine flowers. Alpenrose in particular should be found in midsummer, its bright pink flowers marking its position from some distance across the rocky hillside.

5 ☐   Ignore the signposted path to the right pointing to the Fieger-horn and walk ahead across the minor hillock of Greibühel — 7,375ft (2,247m).

There is a good view of Kals and the lower Kalser valley from Greibühel. It also marks the end of the gradual climb from the Neues Lucknerhaus.

6 ☐   Follow the contours around the head of a south-facing side valley and then climb gently to the top of the Pohleshorn — 7,417ft (2,260m).

Good views of the western wall of the Kalserbach valley open up on the descent from the Pohleshorn.

7 ☐   Turn left away from the summit of the Pohleshorn, downhill and to the south-west along a rocky path. Go beneath the Geier Spitze — 6,899ft (2,102m), towards the upper limits of the pine forest.

8 ☐   Turn sharp right through an arm of the forest, then out onto the open hillside for the last time.

9 ☐   Left into the forest, steeply downhill to a forest road.

10 ☐   Cross two arms of the road, then follow it, by the side of the Burgerbach stream, to the valley road.

There is an old watermill close by the junction with the valley road.

11 ☐   Turn right on the valley road for about 200yd (180m) as far as some farm buildings.

12 ☐   Turn left at the farm to follow a riverside path downstream through meadows along the bank of the Kalserbach , to the west of the hamlet of Burg.

Two more watermills are passed on this stretch.

13 ☐   Turn right along the Grossdorf road. Cross over the Kalser-bach then left at the side of a watermill to join the Grossdorf-Kals road by a chapel.

14 ☐   Follow the road, again passing watermills, all the way back to Kals.

B • THE BLAUSPITZE

8 miles (13km). 4–5 hours. Moderate.
1,867ft (569m) ascent.

In a region of high dramatic mountains, most of them clad by permanent snowfields, the Blauspitze, lowly though it may be by comparison, will give the first-time climber a genuine feeling of achievement on reaching its summit rocks. From this vantage point, the view to the north-east is directly along the steep Freiwand Spitz ridge to the jagged ice falls of the Ködnitzkees and Teischnitkees glaciers, flowing from the final summit rocks of the Grossglockner and its satellites.

Using the short, but useful Glocknerblick chairlift to climb the first 1,989ft (606m), the path beyond it climbs at a steady angle beneath rocky Ganotzkogel — 8,451ft (2,575m) to reach a break in the ridge at the Hocktor col — 8,129ft (2,477m). Turning left the path crosses a series of summits to reach Blauspitze before it gradually loses height into a wide col and the strategically placed Kals-Matreier-Törlhaus hut. At this point, strong walkers can attempt the Roten Kugel — 9,065ft (2,762m) before returning to the col and following the path downhill into forest and eventually back to Kals.

The Route

1 ☐   Take the chairlift from Grossdorf, above Kals, to the Glocknerblick restaurant.

Pause to admire the view, eastwards across the Kalserbach valley. To your left is the Glockner group and right, the Schober group, the latter not so well known as their taller neighbours and with less dramatic glaciers, but worth any number of photographs.

2 ☐   Bear right, uphill across the alpine pasture, along a broad ridge between the upper limits of the pine forest and as far as the group of summer farms at Ganotz Alm.

Ganotz Alm is only used in summer, the animals in age-old tradition, being brought annually from the main farms in the lower valley. Milk from the cattle kept on the high pastures is converted into butter and cheese.

3 ☐   Keep right at Ganotz Alm to follow the signposted Aussig-

The Glockner group

Teplitzer-Weg around a high corrie.

4 ☐   Ignoring a path to the left, climb a rocky slope then around the eastern shoulder of the Ganotzkogel — 8,451ft (2,575m).

5 ☐   Gradually on an easier gradient follow the path, north-westwards, to the Hochtor col — 8,129ft (2,477m). Ignore a path to the left which climbs more steeply, to the crest of the ridge.

Hochtor is a good viewpoint for the Isel valley in the west of the Grossglockner, above the Teischnitzen valley to the east.

6 ☐   Turn left at the col and walk more or less due south, climbing gradually beneath the western slopes of the Weisser Knopf — 8,510ft (2,593m) — to the Blauspitze.

The summit of the Blauspitze — 8,333ft (2,539m) and the highest point reached on this walk, is marked by a large cross, a traditional feature on Austrian and most other alpine summits. Here is an obvious place to pause, admire the view and take photographs.

7 ☐   Follow the rocky path downhill along the grassy ridge across the

minor summits of Presslerkopf — 7,988ft (2,434m), Kalser Hohe — 7,834ft (2,387m) and Feldkopf — 7,457ft (2,272m) into the col.

Flowers enjoy the maximum sunshine of the south-facing ridge.

The Kals-Matreier-Törlhaus will be a welcome sight after crossing the dry mountain ridge.

If time and energy allows, an optional extension would be to continue south along the ridge to climb the Roten Kugel — 9,065ft (2,762m), but this means an extra 1,608ft (490m) ascent and adds about 4'/₂ miles (7.2km) to the route. Return to the col.

8 ☐   Follow the signposted path eastwards and downhill to cross high alpine pasture and into pine forest. The path is signposted as the Weitwanderweg and also to Kals — part of a long-distance trans-Austria footpath.

9 ☐   Continue downhill through forest as far as the northern arm of the Raseckbach. Do not cross the stream, but follow it to the right downstream.

10 ☐   Turn left over the stream and climb up to a forestry road.

11 ☐   Turn right and follow the rough road downhill through alpine meadows. Skirt the southern limits of Grossdorf and walk down to the river, the Kalserbach.

12 ☐   Turn right downstream along the river bank and cross over opposite the church to enter Kals.

C • THE PANORAMAWEG

3¹/₂ miles (5.6km). 2 hours. Easy.

This is a shorter version of the preceeding walk — The Blauspitze — and can be used on either an off day, or perhaps by anyone not wishing to climb the Blauspitze, but who would like to join the rest of their party at the Kals-Matreier-Törlhaus hut.

There is very little climbing on this walk, the height being gained and lost by the use of chairlifts.

To reach the first chairlift it will be necessary to travel by post bus to Matrei in Osttirol, so check the timetable beforehand if intending to meet up with anyone at the Kals-Matreier-Törlhaus.

The Route

1 ☐   Take the post bus from Kals to the centre of Matrei-in-Osttirol and follow the signposts through the suburb of Klaunz to the bottom station of the Goldried chairlift. Use both stages to reach the top.

2 ☐   Follow the signposted Panoramaweg behind the Goldried restaurant and across a stream, the Goldriegelbach.

There is an optional diversion which follows the stream as far as the tiny Goldriedsee, filling a hollow beneath a spur of Gurner —8,868ft (2,702m). If taking this diversion continue to follow the side path to rejoin the main track.

3 ☐   Climb gently to point 2259 and continue around the broad spur on a level path across high alpine pasture.

4 ☐   Reach the alpine hut on the col of Kals-Matreier-Törl.

5 ☐   Still following the Panoramaweg, bear left away from the col, downhill across grassy slopes beneath the Blauspitze.

This is an excellent area for alpine flowers. The views from this slope are superb and take in the Grossglockner giants as well as the Schober group to the south-east.

6 ☐   At the farm buildings on Ganotz Alm, turn right, downhill along a broad ridge bordered by the twin arms of a pine forest.

7 ☐   Take the Glocknerblick chairlift downhill into Grossdorf. It is only a short walk back along the road to Kals, or perhaps a convenient post bus could be used.

D • THE STÜDL HUT

13 miles (21km). 6–8 hours. Strenuous.
4,884ft (1,476m) ascent.

This is quite a tough walk, but taken steadily it is straightforward and well within the capabilities of anyone used to hillwalking at lower altitudes. Its highpoint, in more than one sense, is the Stüdl hut which sits on a col at the end of the Freiwand Spitz's north ridge. To the north a narrow ridge, the Luisengrat, points directly towards the summit of the Grossglockner and on either side of it are steep, south-flowing glaciers.

Below the hut and filling the upper valleys on each side of the Freiwand ridge, lie huge areas of scree and rubble, debris deposited by these glaciers and left behind as they gradually retreated. This rubble, or moraine, has been worn off the slopes of the nearby mountains. The process of grinding down the comparatively young alpine peaks creates the layers which may be raised into mountains millions of years from now; a process which has been occurring since the earth was formed.

The route follows the Ködnitz valley past conveniently sited huts, before climbing to the Stüdl hut, remote on its col. Descending, the path crosses a rocky hillside to the west of the Freiwand Spitz and above the Teischnitz stream, eventually joining the Kaiserbach valley and the possibility of a post bus for the last 2$^1/_2$ miles (4km) back to Kals.

The Route

1 □   Follow the Ködnitz valley walk (A) alongside the Ködnitz river as far as the Neues Lucknerhaus hut.

2 □   Climb along the riverside access road to the bottom stations of two supply cables at point 2063.

The valley sides are steep and create a feeling of being enclosed, which soon goes once the path reaches the Lucknerhaus.

3 □   Cross the stream and climb steeply to the Lucknerhaus.

4 □   Still climbing, reach a footpath junction near a small mountain chapel.

5 ☐ Turn left at the junction and climb the rocky hillside, to reach a gap in the north-facing ridge marked by the Stüdl hut — 9,193ft (2,801m), and the end of the climb.

The views from the hut will make the toil of climbing the Ködnitz valley worthwhile. This is the true high mountain environment.

6 ☐ Turn left, downhill, at first over rocks then out across the boulder-strewn slopes to the west of the Freiwand Spitz. **Take extra care on this section**, a slip could be fatal.

High alpine flowers in this area are mainly tiny cushion plants hiding in the shelter of rocks. They give way to bushier species lower down the valley.

The view ahead is of the lower ramparts of the Granatspitz group of mountains.

7 ☐ Keeping well above the stream, follow the path down the Teischnitz valley as far as the tree line.

8 ☐ Walk downhill on a steep path through the pine forest, into the Kalserbach valley.

9 ☐ Turn left along the valley road and follow it into Kals.

Post buses run along the Kalserbach road as far as the Taurer Hotel.

E • DORFER SEE

14 miles (22.5km). 6–8 hours. Easy.

Even though everyone hopes for fine weather on their alpine holidays there are times when rain spoils any attempt at anything other than valley walking. Here then is a walk for such a day. The route is easy to follow, it simply keeps to the riverside track all the way to the Kalser Tauernhaus, a well placed mountain hut where perhaps if the weather is cold as well as wet, you may want to buy a drink more warming than soup!

An advantage of the route is that if the weather does improve, the walk can be extended to the Dorfer See, the lake filling a hollow left by a retreating glacier which shaped the valley.

The return is by the same route, but should not be a disappointment, because the view will be entirely different — especially if the weather has improved!

The Route

1 ☐   Either take the post bus or walk along the Dorferbach valley as far as the road junction by the Taurer Hotel.

2 ☐   Follow the riverside track through a rocky gorge and beneath ancient pines.

Woodland gives way to tiny alpine meadows bordering the rocky lower crags of nearby mountains. The turbulent stream makes an ideal accompaniment.

3 ☐   Keep along the track opposite the Bergrain Hut, or cross over to it if in need of refreshment.

4 ☐   The valley widens a little and the track passes a series of isolated farmhouses. At this point the river changes its name from the Kalserbach to the Dorferbach.

5 ☐   Reach the Kalser Tauernhaus hut — 5,760ft (1,755m) set among a group of summer farmsteads.

6 ☐   The walk continues beyond the hut, now on a woodland path, to a group of old farms at point 1825.

7 ☐   Continue as far as the Dorfer See and beyond if time and energy allows, but remember that you have to reverse the whole length of the walk to return to Kals.

The hollow filled by the Dorfer See was created by a huge lump of ice which remained on this site long after the parent glacier retreated. Glacial moraine and debris piled up by melt water made a natural dam.

The valley ends at the col of the Kalser Tauern — 8,264ft (2,518m) on the other side of which is the man-made lake of Weissee.

8 ☐   Return by reversing the walk and following the valley downstream to Kals.

F • AROUND THE SCHÖNLEITEN SPITZ

13½ miles (22km). 7–8 hours. Strenuous.
5,455ft (1,662m) ascent.

On no account should this walk be undertaken by anyone who is either ill-prepared or ill-equipped. It is a hard walk, a mountain expedition, but one which will give satisfaction to everyone who completes it. Not only does the route circle the shapely Schönleiten Spitz and its craggy neighbours, but it also climbs alongside a small glacier, the Peischlachkessel Kees (*Kees* is the dialect word for a glacier).

Climbing steeply through forest above Kals, the open hillside is soon gained and a contour-hugging path is followed to a rocky area at the foot of the glacier. The climb then steepens until the col of Tschadinsattel — 9,803ft (2,987m) which is also the highest point of the walk. The Friedrich Senders-Weg path follows a series of steep zigzags down the upper Lesachbach valley and gradually levels out above the welcome sight of the Lasachalm hut. There is a choice of routes from the hut, either along its access track, or following the river to Lesach village. The latter path is the shorter, but tired walkers may prefer the access track.

The Route

1 ☐ Follow the Ködnitz valley track as far as the bend beyond the second watermill. Turn right to cross the river and climb steeply through pine forest on a well marked path.

2 ☐ Cross the open space at Glorergarten Alm.

Pause for a rest by the tiny alpine chapel at Glorergarten Alm.

3 ☐ Continue uphill, ignoring forest drives on either side, until the upper limit of the forest is reached.

4 ☐ Turn left at a footpath junction, now on easier gradients, across the hillside.

5 ☐ Keep walking ahead, now uphill past two footpath junctions.

The climb is made worthwhile by the view across the deep valley to the north and the abundance of alpine flowers.

6 ☐   With rock and scree underfoot, keep ahead at a path junction and then right at the next.

7 ☐   Climb by the foot of the Peischlachkessel glacier as far as the col of Tschadinsattel — 9,803ft (2,987m), the summit of the walk.

Take care if wandering out on to the glacier to examine it at close quarters, the upper section has a number of crevasses which could trap the unwary.

8 ☐   Walk downhill following a series of zigzags into the Lesachbach valley, at first down the boulder-filled hillside, then on easier ground beyond the junction of four streams.

There are excellent views of the northern ridges of the Schober group from the upper Lesachbach valley.

9 ☐   Cross flowery alpine pasture to a group of farmsteads and enter the shady confines of the pine forest.

10 ☐   Reach the Lasachalm hut.

11 ☐   Follow the riverside path downstream along its left bank and through dense pine forest, offering shade at the end of a long walk.

12 ☐   Cross the river below an old mill at Rubisoi and continue downstream into Ober Lesach.

13 ☐   Turn right by the upper houses, across the access road to follow a path at first across the open hillside, then into forest for the last time.

14 ☐   Continue downhill as far as the valley road which is joined conveniently near the Café Tyrol.

15 ☐   Turn right and follow the road into Kals.

G • **FRANZ-JOSEPH HÖHE** (2-day Walk)

28 miles (45km). 14–16 hours. Strenuous.

Here is an introductory walk to high-level alpine hut-to-hut touring; 28 miles to be spread over 2 days. Franz-Joseph, the Emperor of the Austro-Hungarian Empire came as far as this point in his attempt on the highest mountain in his realm. Of course, at that time there was not a well made motor road and no doubt the glacier came much lower. His memorial stands high above the valley and an hotel bears his name.

There are at least eight establishments offering accommodation at the foot of the Pasterzen glacier, so where you stay depends upon price and also the availability of rooms. It is therefore recommended that a telephone booking is made in advance — the tourist office in Kals should be able to help in this direction.

Two ridges must be crossed on the way out and back, and the climbing is accordingly steep, but the route is interesting throughout and the excitement on reaching the foot of the Pasterzen glacier makes the effort worthwhile.

On the outward leg, the route repeats part of the climb along the Ködnitz valley as followed on the Stüdl hut walk (D) before crossing a rocky ridge below the Blaue Kopf. Across the Leitertal valley, a high-level path, the Weiner Hohenweg, skirts the dramatic lower crags of the Schwertkopf and then descends to the Stausee Margaritze and its views favoured by the former Emperor Franz-Joseph.

After an overnight stay , a lower path is used for the return, at first along the north bank, upstream, of the Leiter river, crossing to climb by the Glatz stream to the Glorer hut and then downhill all the way back to Kals.

There are several tourist attractions around the lower part of the Pasterzen glacier, so allow time to explore it in full.

The Route

1 ☐ Follow the steep track up the Ködnitztal as described in the Stüdl hut walk as far as a mountain shrine below the valley head.

2 ☐ Turn right and follow the contours around the slopes of the Lange Wand, the south ridge of Blaue Kopf.

3 ☐ Cross the narrow col of Pfortscharte and walk steeply across a

boulder-strewn hillside into the Leitertal.

4 ☐ Cross the Leiterbach and climb up to the Salm hut.

5 ☐ Take the left-hand path, the Weiner Hohenweg, and follow its contour-hugging course along the mountainside.

6 ☐ Turn left through the narrow gap of the Stocker Scharte — 8,014ft (2,442m).

7 ☐ Steeply downhill to the Stausee Margaritze.

Awe-inspiring ice fields and towering peaks reach towards the sky as you cross the valley by the side of the lake. On a day with no wind the view is mirrored in its still waters.

8 ☐ Climb up to the road and your chosen accommodation for the night.

Spend time exploring the glacier and in the evening watch the upper slopes turn a rosy pink with the setting sun.

9 ☐ For the return, walk down to the Stausee Margaritze following the same path as the previous day, but turn left on the path which crosses the rocky Dursenwand. Follow it into the valley bottom.

10 ☐ Turn right, upstream along the north bank of the Leiter river.

11 ☐ Take the second path across the valley and climb steeply up the side valley of the Glatz.

12 ☐ Pause at the Glorer hut — 8,671ft (2,642m).

13 ☐ Take the left-hand path, following the contours around the hillside beneath Kasteneck — 9,268ft (2,824m) as far as a path 'crossroads' at Peischlach Törl — 8,172ft (2,490m).

14 ☐ Turn right by the shrine which marks the col and walk downhill above the Peischlach stream.

15 ☐ Zigzag away from the valley into the farmstead of Wiggalm.

16 ☐ Follow the access track into the forest.

17 ☐ Turn left along the Ködnitztal road to reach Kals.

H • HASLACH

4 miles (6.4km). 2 hours. Easy.

This is a walk for, say, the last evening, or after a day spent sightseeing or shopping. It is easy to follow as it parallels the main road out of Kals. Unless you have time to spare, the best way to do the walk would be to take the post bus or a taxi down to Haslach and walk back to Kals.

The Route

1 □   Take the post bus to Haslach and walk back along the road for about ¹/₄ mile (0.4km).

2 □   Climb the zigzag path across a meadow and into the forest.

3 □   Keep right across the hillside as far as the hamlet of Arnig.

4 □   Take the left fork away from Arnig and follow the lane, past a watermill and up to the main road.

5 □   Turn left away from the road, following the Kalser river through forest and later across open meadows.

6 □   Cross the river a little way above Café Tyrol.

7 □   Follow the east bank until Kals church comes into view, then turn right to reach the village.

Turk's Head Lily grows wild in the Tyrol

9 LIENZ

Map

Kompass Wanderkarte (1:50,000 series) Sheet 47; Lienzer Dolomiten.

How to Get There

Road

1 • Direct Route South-east across Europe by the motorway system to Munich; continue on *Autobahn* number 8 (E11) and number 93 (E86) to Kufstein. East to St Johann, then south via Kitzbühel to Mittersill. East to Bruck and south via the Felber Tauern Tunnel into the Insel valley to Lienz.

2 • For a detour via Salzburg, south-west along the Salzach valley to Kitzbühel, then as route **1**.

3 • As **1** as far as Bruck (to the east of Zell am See) and south by the scenically awe-inspiring Grossglockner Road to Heiligenblut and Lienz.

Note It must be made clear that the Grossglockner route **3** described above is arduous on both drivers and heavily laden cars. The route via Mittersill and the Felber Tauern Tunnel route may be longer, but is far less tiring.

Rail

1 • Trans-European Services via Innsbruck and the Brenner Pass to Bressanone (Brixen) in northern Italy, and then on the Carinthia line via Dobbiaco to Lienz.

2 • South from Salzburg on the Klagenfurt (Carinthia) line. Change at Spittal for the Lienz train.

Air

Nearest international airports are at Innsbruck, Klagenfurt and Salzburg. Rail or bus connections.

The Area

The region is steeped in ancient history, the Romans built an important east-west road between northern Italy and Carinthia, following an even older route used by a civilisation in what is known to archaeologists as the Hallstatt period.

There are still extensive remains of the Roman town between modern Nussdorf and Dölsach, under 3 miles (5km) to the east of Lienz. Known as Aguntum it was an important market, or more correctly trading centre, for the Hallstatt people even before the Romans came.

Lienz is at the junction of three valleys. The Isel is to the north-west, the main Drau valley to the east and Pustertal to the west, although it is the river Drau which flows along the latter, the ancient east–west route referred to above.

To the south of Lienz are the dramatic limestone peaks of the Lienzer Dolomiten, the north-eastern ramparts of the main range, mostly confined to northern Italy, known generally as the Dolomites. To the immediate north and west of the town, easier but equally high mountains line the three valleys.

Further north, beyond the local mountains is the massive wall of rock and ice which marks the boundary between Ost Tirol and Salz-burgland. Here is the home of Austria's highest peaks; directly north of Lienz and skirted by the high-level road to Zell am See, is the Grossglockner Massif — 12,461ft (3,797m), the summit of Austria, and further west is the Grossvenediger — 12,058ft (3,674m) and its satellites. Both mountain ranges are accessible from motor roads running north from Lienz.

The town itself has much to offer the tourist, either as a base for exploring the nearby mountains, or simply as a relaxing holiday venue. Quite large by Tirolean standards, it has over 10,000 inhabitants living in the town and surrounding villages. Of course, that number is considerably swollen during the holidays, however it never seems to be overcrowded and the mountains are always places of complete freedom.

Lieburg Palace, a grand confection in the main square, dates from the sixteenth century, now fulfilling a more prosaic use as the regional administrative headquarters. The parish church is fifteenth century; four magnificent late Gothic winged altars act as focal points and the frescoes are by Albin Egger-Lienz, a famous religious artist, who is also buried in this church.

Schloss Bruck guards the entrance to the Isel valley, a mile outside the town to the west, once commanding movement in this part of Austria. Once the seat of the powerful Görf family, it has a fine museum of local artifacts and Roman remains found nearby, as well as paintings by Egger-Lienz and Franz Defregger, another local artist.

The well preserved castle dates from the thirteenth century, but most of the present structure is sixteenth century. Its best features are the central tower and the Romanesque chapel decorated with late fifteenth-century frescoes.

Other attractions in Lienz are its sheltered lido, an ideal place on a hot summer's day, especially after a brisk walk. Golf, tennis and boating on the Tristacher See beneath the forested shoulders of the Rauchkofel will claim the attention of walkers and non-walkers alike.

Hillwalking is as varied as one would wish, from high-level ridges and peak storming, to more gentle valley and forest strolling. A chairlift and a cabin lift climb the lower slopes on two sides of Lienz to make an easy and quick way of gaining height on to the Hochstein and Zettersfeld mountains.

Useful Information

Local Tourist Office
Fremdenverkehrsverband
Lienzer Dolomiten
Albin-Egger Strasse 17
A9900 Linz/Osttirol
☎ (04852) 4747

Accommodation
Everything from top class hotels to rented accommodation and bed and breakfast. Several camp sites in Lienz and the surrounding villages. One youth hostel.

Cable Cars and Chairlifts
Schlossberg Two chairlifts, the lower starting on the western outskirts of Lienz which climbs to Taxen and the second stage is to Sternalm.
Zettersfeld Cable car from Gratendorf, north of Lienz centre to the southern slopes of the Zettersfeld.

Recommended Local Excursions
Carinthian Lake District and Klagenfurt To the east via Villach, on any of the minor valley routes as well as by the main road.
Grossglockner road (toll) High-level motor road to the east of Austria's highest mountain.
Schloss Bruck Folk museum in the well preserved thirteenth/sixteenth-century castle to the west of Lienz.

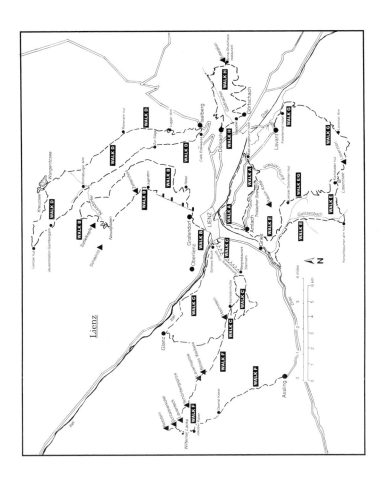

Lienz

WALK D
WALK B
WALK H
WALK A
WALK E
WALK G
WALK C
WALK F

Wangenitzsee
Kreuzsee
Lienzer hut
Jaulalenstation Gamsgrube
Dolomitenhutte
Dornauberger Alm
Moosalm hut
Luggar Alm
Zur Steig
Café Edelweiss
Isselsberg
Dölsach
Göriach
Gödnach
Göttschbach
Wienerhutte/Gasthaus Ausserst Schutzhaus restaurant
Drau
Lavant
Forchheid Hotel
Kreithof
Jauchner Alm
Kerschbaumer Alm hut
Lavanter Alm
Kerschbaumer hut
Lasörling
Lienzer Dolomiten hut
Tristacher See
Jauch Kofel
Kristlamboch
Galitzenbach
Amlach
Gries
LIENZ
Grafendorf
Oberlienz
Schloss Bruck
Bergrestaurant Steinalm
Anschönaumhütte
Kreithof
Kaapenfor
Zetterfeld
Siesar
Stanedorfa
Schleinitz
NeualBauern
Glanz
Assling
Jokerhütte
Mariener Wiese
Gödinger
Schossbergspitze
Ederplan Kaser
Willener Lacken
Kerschbaum
Rosstein

4 miles
6 km

N

A • TRISTACHER SEE

6 miles (10km). 3 hours. Easy. 453ft (138m) climb.

This is a relatively simple and straightforward walk without any difficult climbing. It is an ideal first day walk, or for a half day if the rest of the time is required for other plans. Alternatively the Tristacher See at the 'crux' of the walk could make an attractive venue, on a short easy woodland ramble linked to either a bathe or gentle boat ride on the tree-shrouded waters of the lake.

Basically, the route is south, upstream along the Drau then east uphill through the little village of Amlach. Woodland walking leads to the lake, then downhill into the main valley. A riverside track leads back, steadily upstream to Lienz.

The Route

1 ☐   From the town centre follow the signposts across the river to the swimming pool (*Hallenbad*).

2 ☐   Turn right and walk upstream on the side road, past the swimming pool. Walk with the river on your right and hay meadows on the left.

Above the bridge an old watermill links the busy tourist town with days when locals would bring their grain to the mill to be ground into flour.

3 ☐   At the next bridge, do not cross, but bear left alongside and then into a small pine wood.

4 ☐   Walk through the village of Amlach and out on the Tristach road.

A couple of Gasthöfe *in Amlach will offer morning coffee. The church is worth a short diversion.*

5 ☐   Fork right in front of Pension Laserz and climb uphill beyond the fields and into pine forest on the Tristacher See road.

6 ☐   About $\frac{1}{2}$ mile (1km) beyond the Pension Laserz turning, go right, away from the direction of the road and on to a minor forest road.

7 ☐   Follow the road, uphill through the silent pine woods, bearing left beneath the lower craggy slopes of the Rauchkofel.

8 ☐   Walk down to the Tristacher See. A sandy path follows its shoreline and will make a pleasant, short addition to the walk.

The Tristacher See is a series of small pond-like waters leading into the main lake. There is a restaurant, picnic areas, swimming (it is usual to pay for outdoor bathing in semi-commercialised lakes such as the Tristacher See), pedalo boating, or simply take in the pleasant mountain atmosphere.

9 ☐   Walk away, eastwards from the lake, keeping right at a complex junction of tracks. Follow the route of a toboggan run, a forest road in summer, uphill to a small stream.

10 ☐   Turn left and follow the stream, the Kohlstattbach, downhill to a group of farm buildings and the Bad Jungbrunn Hotel.

11 ☐   Walk to the right of a small chapel and across the valley road.

12 ☐   Go over a series of meadows to the south bank of the river Drau.

Notice how the river has had to be controlled by straightening and raising its banks to cope with the massive volume of water which rushes down the valley after every winter.

13 ☐   Turn left and follow an easy track alongside the river, first through pine forest and later across meadowland near the junction of the Drau with the Isel.

14 ☐   Join a minor road and follow it back over the river and into the main part of Lienz.

B • NEUALPSEEN

9 miles (14km). 5 hours. Moderate.
2,137ft (651m) ascent.

The twin lakes, the Neualpseen, are in complete contrast to the Tris-tacher See. Where the latter is secluded forest water, the Neualpseen are real mountain lakes. Set on a high rocky plateau and filled by meltwater from winter snows, they are perfect examples. To the north and west are the craggy slopes of the Sattelkopfe and Schleinitz, two attractive mountains to tempt any budding alpinist with energy to spare after reaching the lakes. Lovers of alpine flowers will enjoy wandering amongst the rocks and tiny grassy patches of the lower hillsides and also the plateau near the lakes, as well as the upper slopes above the tree line of Debanttal.

By using the cable car from Grafendorf to its highest point, most of the height required for this walk is gained without effort. A steady climb leads to a rocky, but easy ridge. Beyond it is the plateau and its hollow filled by the Neualpseen. A short scramble is necessary to reach a fairly steep downhill section, but later an easier path leads across the hillside, then down into the Debanttal forest. A forest track, improving to a metalled hillside road, leads the walker back along the valley to Lienz.

The Route

1 ☐ Walk through the northern outskirts of Lienz, uphill towards the village of Grafendorf.

2 ☐ Take the cable car to the upper limits of the forest.

3 ☐ Walk uphill to the mountain youth hostel at Happ Wiesen (signposted to A.V. Jugendheim).

4 ☐ Follow a fairly steep path uphill to the summit of Zettersfeld — 7,263ft (2,213m).

Pause by the summit cross to admire the view of the Lienzer Dolomiten range to the south, across the valley.

5 ☐ Keep to the left of the ridge (as seen when facing it) and go left again at two footpath junctions. The going underfoot is rocky at this point.

174

6 ☐   At a small cross, turn right, steeply down to the twin lakes of the Neualpseen — 7,995ft (2,436m).

The lakes make an attractive place to spend an hour (if time permits) either looking at the scenery, or at the masses of alpine flowers growing in the surrounding rocks. Swimming in the icy waters is for hardy types only.

The summits to the north-west which dominate this little hollow are Sattelkopfe — 8,700ft (2,651m) to the north, and Schleinitz — 9,534ft (2,905m).

7 ☐   Follow a rocky path northwards, across the upper valley which drains the Neualpseen.

8 ☐   Go round the east shoulder of Sattelkopfe, then steeply downhill on rocky ground into the Trelebitschbach valley.

9 ☐   Turn right at a path junction by an old farmhouse.

10 ☐   Follow the slanting track downhill through sparse pine forest, over the Nussdorfer stream.

11 ☐   At a path crossing marked by a wayside cross, turn left past an old farm and into the main forest.

12 ☐   Bear right on a path where a road starts to descend on the left.

13 ☐   Cross a couple of clearings and join the forest road.

14 ☐   Turn right along a trackway and follow it until it eventually joins the metalled road.

15 ☐   Go downhill along the road through Gainberg and Grafendorf villages into Lienz.

Restaurants and small Gasthöfe *on the roadside will make the last and longest leg of the journey less arduous.*

C • HOCHSTEIN

10¹/₂ miles (17km). 5–6 hours. Moderate.
1,500ft (457m) ascent, 4,493ft (1,369m) descent.

The Hochstein is a popular vantage point to the west of Lienz. Overlooking all three valleys, the view covers most of East Tyrol and part of Carinthia to the east. To the north stretches the Grossglockner and Venediger ranges, a spectacular view which needs a clear day. Ideally the best time is early morning, but that is not always possible unless you can make an alpine start or drive up the toll road at first light. Probably the best way to appreciate the view is to keep an eye on the weather and choose a cloudless, but not too hazy, day for this expedition.

Most of the height is gained by using the two stages of the Schlossberg chairlift. Easy tracks climb the forested hillside to a mountain road which is then followed as far as the Hochstein hut. Leaving the forest behind, an easy ridge is crossed, then a side path drops towards the village of Glanz in the Isel valley. Turning right at Glanz, a quiet lane leads back towards Lienz following an easy route through meadows on the right bank of the river.

The Route

1 ☐   Follow the road out of Lienz centre towards Schloss Bruck and the folk museum.

2 ☐   Take both stages of the Schlossberg chairlift to the final station.

3 ☐   Bear left at Bergrestaurant Sternal along a woodland track.

4 ☐   Ahead and uphill at a track crossing. Ignore side tracks and footpaths, but climb steadily by the forest track.

5 ☐   Join the access road, turn right and follow it as far as the Hochsteinhütte restaurant. Leave the forest prior to reaching the restaurant.

The Hochsteinhütte is a busy restaurant reached either by foot or car along its toll road, it is highly recommended.

6 ☐   Turn right in front of the restaurant to follow a signposted footpath to the summit of the Hochstein.

Hochstein — 6,751ft (2,057m), as mentioned in the introduction to

Mountain pastures near Lienz

---

this walk, is a fine viewpoint.

7 □   Walk ahead along the broad ridge, skirting rocky outcrops as may be necessary from time to time.

8 □   Bear right at a path junction and go downhill away from the crest of the ridge.

9 □   Skirt the upper limits of the pine forest. Pass a prominently situated cross on the Wetterkreuz spur.

10 □   Join a farm access track at Koch Alm.

11 □   Follow the signposted path to the right, steeply downhill on alpine meadowland, crossing an access track below a farmstead.

12 □   Cross a small stream and climb up to the forest.

13 □   Zigzag within the pine forest. Cross a track and bear left, downhill to the village of Glanz.

14 □   Turn right in front of the church and walk away from the village along its road. Go down towards the River Isel.

15 □   On reaching the river do not cross the bridge, but turn right along a farm lane.

16 ☐ Go through riverside meadowland as far as a bridge opposite the village of Oberlienz.

17 ☐ Again do not cross the bridge, but turn right to follow a minor path back to Lienz, joining the valley road beneath the castle.

If time permits, the end of the walk can be combined with a visit to the Heimatmuseum (Folk Museum) at Schloss Bruck. Also look out for the delightful old watermill on the riverbank below the castle.

D • WANGENITZSEE

17 miles (27km). 8–10 hours. Strenuous.
5,136ft (1,565m) climb.

This is a long hard walk which also involves considerably more climbing on foot than most of the others in this guide. However, the height is gained gradually and apart from the last climb from the Lienzer hut to the Wangenitzsee, nowhere else is it excessively steep.

The route follows the Debant valley almost to its source, using a quiet forest track which is never far from a noisy stream. Clearings along the way break the monotony of forest walking. From the Lienzer hut, a rocky path (the Zinkeweg) climbs to the Wangenitzsee and its neighbour the Franzsee, two mountain lakes set in rocky hollows. Beyond, the way is gradually downhill on a steadily improving track which leads along the forested Penzelberg ridge and then drops steeply into the village of Iselsberg.

In Iselsberg a choice of *Gasthöfe* offer refreshment before catching the bus back along the short stretch of motor road into Lienz.

The Route

1 ☐ Either catch the local post bus along the Iselsberg road out of Lienz or drive to Café Edelweiss.

2 ☐ Follow the lane away from the café across a short stretch of meadowland and into the pine forest.

3 ☐ Walk down to the river and cross over. Turn right at a track junction in front of the Zur Säge *Gasthof.*

4 ☐　Pass above an old watermill and then recross the river. Continue upstream along its true left bank (the river should be on your left at this point).

5 ☐　Follow the forest track, which is interspersed with occasional small clearings, towards a junction of tracks below a group of summer farms at Domaburger Alm. Cross the river and turn right still upstream.

Several small pools, natural widenings in the streambed, make tempting bathing places, but unless the walk is to be curtailed, time will not allow many stops along the way.

6 ☐　Either call in or pass the Jausenstation Gaimbergalm on a small hillock in the centre of a clearing.

7 ☐　Leave the trees, which by now have thinned out, and enter the valley's mountain zone.

8 ☐　The Lienzer hut — 6,489ft (1,977m) marks the end of valley walking. Turn right and cross the headwaters of the river.

9 ☐　Climb the rocky hillside, bearing right above a series of crags, the Schwalbenwand.

10 ☐　Cross a side stream below point 2021 and follow the uphill waymarked path, the Zinkeweg, which becomes easier.

11 ☐　Ignore a side path and bear left, steeply now and zigzag uphill beneath an supply cable to the Wangenitzsee hut.

12 ☐　Reach the Wangenitzsee.

Kreuzsee is to the left, slightly higher than Wangenitzsee. The Mountain hut situated on the north bank of the lake could be used for an overnight stop in an emergency. In any case it will be an obvious place to call for refreshment before continuing the walk.

13 ☐　Bear left away from the lake downhill on the rocky path of the Weiner Hohenweg.

14 ☐　At the Raneralm hut an access track leads downhill along the crest of a broad ridge. Follow it past a series of small farmsteads.

15 ☐　Turn right at Lugger Alm, steeply downhill and into pine forest.

16 ☐　There are several paths available on the last steep section, all lead on to Iselsberg.

17 ☐　Either catch the bus back to Lienz or walk the short length of road, downhill to the car park at the Café Edelweiss.

E • KERSCHBAUMERALM AND THE KARLSBADER HUT

13½ miles (22km). 8 hours. Strenuous.
5,038ft (1,535m) climb.

Here is a mountaineering expedition rather than a simple stroll, but it is one which should be within the capabilities of anyone used to hillwalking. The going is strenuous almost every step of the way, especially on the downhill section from the Kerschbaumer Törl col to the Karlsbader hut. Downhill walking should never be looked upon as an easy respite, for as in the case of this walk, downhill can be difficult and needs special care, especially over steep and rocky ground.

The walk starts by the camp site at Gries in the Pustertal valley of the Upper Drau. It follows the access track along the Kerschbaumertal to a well sited mountain hut. A stiff climb reaches the Kerschbaumer Törl and then downhill a little way before the welcome Karlsbader hut comes into view. Easy downhill walking along the access track reaches the Lienzer Dolomiten hut where a double fork links with a downhill path through forest to Amlach.

The Route

1 □   Begin the walk at the bus stop nearest to the camp site at Gries.

2 □   Walk under the railway bridge and turn left off the road. Cross the river and join a minor road at the side of a bridge.

3 □   Turn right and almost immediately cross a bridge over a side stream. Follow a gravel surfaced track, the Stadtweg, uphill through mature pine forest.

4 □   Follow the Galitzenbach upstream. Ignore side tracks and keep to the same side of the river, which should be to your left.

5 □   Leave the upper stunted limits of the forest and enter the high rocky pasture zone.

The rough pasture below the Kerschbaumeralm hut is usually filled with colourful alpine flowers.

6 □   Reach the welcome Schutzhaus Kerschbaumerain hut and pause awhile.

7 ☐   Take the easterly path to the left, away from the hut and cross a small side stream.

8 ☐   Climb steeply by zigzags beyond a small clump of trees. Ignore paths left and right.

9 ☐   Cross the col and then go downhill, with great care, towards the Karlsbader hut.

10 ☐   Follow the path downhill away from the hut eventually into pine forest.

11 ☐   Go past the Lienzer Dolomiten hut and turn left away from the road.

There is an occasional bus service to the Lienzer Dolomiten hut which could be used to shorten the walk at this point, if necessary. Check the timetable beforehand by enquiring at the tourist information office in Lienz.

12 ☐   Walk towards a clearing and turn left at a fork.

13 ☐   Follow the path downhill through pine forest.

14 ☐   Bear right at a footpath junction and go round the rocky western shoulder of the Rauchkofel.

15 ☐   Join a minor road in the valley bottom at Goggkreuz and turn right.

16 ☐   Walk through Amlach village and take the riverside track out towards Lienz.

17 ☐   Go past the swimming pool and left over the river bridge and into the town centre.

F • THE LAVANT RIDGEWALK

11$\frac{1}{2}$ miles (19km). 6–7 hours. Strenuous.
3,925ft (1,196m) climb.

Providing the ridge is snow free, the weather fine, and you and your party have the ability to cope with a little scrambling, this should be an exciting and entertaining ridgewalk.

The walk is an extension to the Hochstein walk (C) and if the walks in this section have been followed in sequence, you should be fit enough to enjoy this one.

The Schlossberg chairlifts will carry you high on the hillside, where an alternative path to the one used in walk C, leads quickly uphill to the Hochstein viewpoint. Beyond it, the ridge leads over a series of interesting peaks, culminating in the summit of Rotstein — 8,848ft (2,696m). From the summit, a short but steep scree slope leads directly into the Wilferner valley where a steadily improving track follows the stream, the Thaler Bach, down to Assling. Buses run from Assling to Lienz. Check the timetable before setting out; you can obtain details at the tourist information office in Lienz.

The Route

1 □   Climb Schlossberg's forested slopes by the twin chairlift.

2 □   Turn right at the cross tracks beyond the Sternalm restaurant.

3 □   Beyond a double bend, turn left uphill on a narrow path.

4 □   Climb through the forest, crossing two forest tracks on the way.

5 □   Bear right at a path junction and go uphill to the Hochsteinhütte restaurant.

6 □   Go past the restaurant and follow the path uphill to the summit of the Hochstein — 6,751ft (2,057m).

7 □   Follow the ridge path to a junction and go left uphill over increasingly rocky terrain.

8 □   Cross the first summit, the Böses Weibele — 8,274ft (2521m).

9 □   Continue along the narrow rocky ridge over the twin summits of the Lavantspitze — 8,353ft (2,545m).

A path to the left beyond the Hinter Lavantspitze could be used to shorten this walk if conditions do not encourage plans to follow the complete route. Take great care on the descent into the Wilferner valley. The track in the valley bottom leads to Assling.

10 ☐ Cross a shaly col and climb the Schönbergspitze — 8,658ft (2,638m).

11 ☐ Follow the waymarked path over Lavanteck — 8,723ft (2,658m) and the Schlaitnerkofel — 8,695ft (2,650m).

12 ☐ Climb the final rocky and scree-covered slopes to the Rotstein — 8,846ft (2,696m).

13 ☐ Turn sharp left from the summit and with great care go down the screes of the south face.

Pause to admire the view at the Wilferner Lacke pool.

14 ☐ Go down to the stream and join a better path starting from an old mountain farmhouse at Jakober Kaser.

15 ☐ Follow the path as far as a valley access track. Leave the latter by turning left at Obertal Kaser hillfarm.

16 ☐ Continue with the now widening stream, the Thaler Bach, on your left. Follow it through dense pine forest, a complete contrast to the exposed ridge above.

Look out for old watermills in the lower reaches of the valley.

17 ☐ Join a road and go down into Assling to catch the bus back to Lienz.

G • THE DREITÖRLWEG

9 miles (14km). 5–6 hours. Moderate/Strenuous.
2,878ft (877m) ascent, 5,980ft (1,822m) descent.

The peaks of the Lienzer Dolomiten rise in a towering white wall, to the south of Lienz. By following the route described for this walk, it is possible to reach the foot of these fantastic mountains. Gigantic peaks rise vertically from their screes to jagged skyline ridges; more amazing when one realises that these rocks were made from myriads of sea creatures which died millions of years ago.

  A bus ride to the Lienzer Dolomiten hut gains about 3,058ft (932m) of the initial climb from the valley bottom and as a result the rest of the way is only a further climb of 2,878ft (877m) in order to reach the Laserztörl col. Steady downhill walking, at first on a scree slope, leads into the Frauenbach valley and from there an easy road leads into Lavant and a convenient bus service.

The Route

1 □ Take an early bus from Lienz to the Lienzer Dolomiten hut.

2 □ Follow the valley track away from the hut and uphill through sparse forest, then out on to high alpine meadows to the Karlsbader hut.

3 □ Turn left away from the hut, past the Laserzsee and climb the scree slopes towards the crags of Laserzkar.

4 □ Follow waymarks around rocky outcrops to the col at Laserztörl — 8,195ft (2,497m), the highest point and crux of the walk.

5 □ Go downhill across a wide scree slope to a wayside cross at a path junction.

Pause to admire the vertical walls of the nearby peaks.

6 □ Turn left at the path junction, downhill to a second junction, again marked by a cross.

7 □ Go to the left, downhill through sparse pine forest into the Frauenbach valley.

8 □ Below Lavanter Alm the path zigzags over rocky ground. Keep to its course to make the walk easy.

9 □ Cross an old treeless avalanche zone, and then into dense pine forest.

10 □ Join an access track and swing to the left across the northern spur of the Lavanter Kolben.

11 □ Ignore a side track going left, but continue downhill.

12 □ Join another access track and turn left.

13 □ Walk through forest clearings, past the turning to the Forellenhof Hotel and go down to the road.

14 □ Turn left into Lavant where there is a bus route back to Lienz.

H • THE ANNA-SCHUTZHAUS

---

8 miles (13km). 5–6 hours. Moderate.
4,345ft (1,324m) climb.

This is a short and pleasant climb from the rural charm of Dölsach to reach the Anna-Schutzhaus at its highest point.

Keeping to forest tracks for most of the way, this is an ideal walk for a rainy day or hot sunny day when shade is required.

The Route

1 ☐   The walk starts in Dölsach village to the east of Lienz and a little to the north of the main valley road. It is served by a regular bus route and there is usually ample car parking if this is required.

2 ☐   Follow the side road across the Gödnacher Bach valley into Gödnach.

Spare a little time to admire the splendid architecture of the churches in these tiny villages.

3 ☐   Continue on and into Görtschach.

4 ☐   Turn left in the village square, uphill on an easy track at first through hay meadows and later through pine forest.

5 ☐   Follow signposts and waymarks to the Anna-Schutzhaus restaurant.

A short diversion behind the restaurant leads to the summit of Ederplan 6,764ft (2,061m), an excellent viewpoint for the Lienzer Dolomites to the south on the opposite side of the main valley.

6 ☐   Turn left from the restaurant, downhill through forest, zigzagging as dictated by the path, where the slope is steep.

7 ☐   Join a valley track following the Gödnacher Bach . Turn left and follow the track downhill.

8 ☐   Turn right across the river, go past isolated farmsteads and walk steadily downhill, mainly through forest.

9 ☐   Bear left by a mill at a road junction and walk down to Dölsach village.

10 RAMSAU

Map

Kompass Wanderkarte (1:50,000 series) Sheet 31; Radstadt-Schladming. Or Kompass Wanderkarte (1:25,000 series) — Ramsau-Dachstein.

How to Get There

Road

1 • East on the German *Autobahn* system via Munich to Salzburg. South on the E14 to Radstadt. East by road 308 to Schladming. Ramsau is to the north along a minor road.

2 • As above to Salzburg then south-east on road 158 to Bad Ischl. Road 145 to Trauenfels, then 308 to Schladming. An optional diversion via Hallstatt can be made by leaving the 145 at St Agatha and rejoining the main road near Bad Aussee.

Rail

Main line Trans-European service via Salzburg or Innsbruck to Bischofshofen and Schladming. Post bus to Ramsau.

Air

The nearest international airport is at Salzburg. Frequent rail connections as above.

The Area

One of the characteristic features of limestone areas in the mountains of Austria, are high-level plateaux above the main valleys. Ramsau sits on one of these ledges, about 1,083ft (330m) above Schladming and the Enns valley. Backed by the massive ramparts of the Dachstein range and facing due south, with the added advantage of a low ridge between it and the final slopes down to Schladming, Ramsau is in an excellent position to make the most of every hour of sunshine. The mountain range and the forested ridge shelter the village from everything but the most persistent weather.

The choice of walking areas is varied. Immediate to the village are a series of easy field and woodland tracks which can be used to create a number of short easy walks. The Dachstein itself, accessible by an almost vertical cable car journey from the road end, offers an exciting yet safe glacier walk followed by a visit to an attractive mountain hut set on a high alp. South of the Enn valley and above Schladming, the high pastures and ridges can be reached by way of the Planei gondola lift. High-level walking above Planei takes in the Hochstein range, providing hard walking, suitable for those with a good head for heights and used to fairly long days on the high fells.

Until haymaking time the meadows surrounding the village are ablaze with a kaleidoscope of flowers which return year after year. The roadsides also have their own shade-loving plants, but it is perhaps the mountainsides and highest alpine meadows where the prettiest flowers are found. These are the tiny cushion plants such as saxifrages, or dwarf gentians and the graceful anemones, all plants which live in an apparently precarious situation sheltered amongst rocks or damp places, all seeking the maximum sunlight.

On non-walking days, visits can easily be arranged to the nearby Hallstatt Salt Mines on the opposite side of the Dachstein range, or to Salzburg and its attractions.

The local tourist office in Ramsau will have details of the walking badge which is awarded against a collection of stamps from local huts and restaurants. A simple but lasting memento of a walking holiday in the area.

Useful Information

Tourist Office
Verkehrsverein
A-8972 Ramsau am Dachstein
☎ 0 36 87/81925 and 81833

Accommodation
Full range of hotel accommodation and *Gasthöfe.* Also rented accommodation and mountain huts (Austrian Alpine Club membership recommended).
Nearest camp site at Schladming (near bypass to the north of the town.)

Cable Cars and Chairlifts
Dachstein Cable Car From Türldwandhütte to the Schladminger glacier Bergstation on the Hune Scharte.
Reiteralmlift Chairlift (two-stage lift) From Gleiming to Reiteralm

Walking in the Dachstein mountains near Ramsau

hut. Gleiming is about 9½ miles (6km) to the west of Schladming.
Planei Gondola Lift From Schladming to the Schladminger Hütte.
Krummholzhütte Lift From Haus to the Krummholzhütte

Glacier Viewing
Both the Hallstatt and Schladminger glaciers are accessible from the
top of the Dachstein cable car. Glacier tours across the Schladminger
are organised throughout the summer season. Check details at the
Ramsau tourist office. English speaking walkers may prefer to follow
walk D below, which crosses this safe glacier by a waymarked route.
A *langlauf* (cross-country skiing) course is kept open throughout the
summer. The lower reaches of the Hallstatt glacier to the north are
heavily crevassed and unsafe for inexperienced mountaineers.

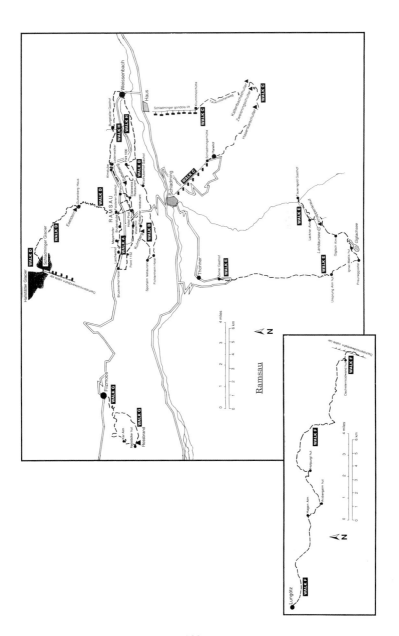

A • THE UPPER RAMSAU VALLEY

$7^1/_2$ miles (12km). 3–4 hours. Easy.

The scattered farmsteads surrounding the central village of Ramsau sit in the sunny upper valley of the Ramsau stream, a tributary of the Enns, eventually joining the Danube (Donau) west of Linz.

Gradients on this walk are easy and generally short. The walk is therefore ideal for the first day in the area. Views are wide ranging and will give a clear introduction to the nearby forested ridges and the steep walls of Dachstein's south face.

The walk begins outside the tourist office in Ramsau and follows the keep-fit course downstream, by the side of the Ramsau Bach. Crossing over to the other side of the valley it follows a well marked route, to the west, past a series of *Gasthöfe* and hotels, all offering refreshment. It then swings back to the south side of the valley and follows the tree-shaded Philosophenweg back to the village.

The Route

1 ☐   Turn right between the tourist office and Hotel Post. Follow the road for about 120yd (110m).

2 ☐   Turn left through trees at the *Fitnessparcours* sign and follow the right-hand bank of the river, the Ramsau Bach.

Fitnessparcours *are keep-fit courses laid out with a series of sign-posted activities. Graded information helps the participant calculate his or her ability and the idea is to jog round the course daily timing oneself or increasing the number of times each activity is carried out.*

3 ☐   Ignore the first of two paths to the left. Take the second across meadowland towards a small wood. Go through it towards the road.

4 ☐   Cross the road and bear left, uphill through a pine wood as far as Kalcher farm.

5 ☐   Skirt the edge of the forested slopes of the Kalchwand and cross the access road to Faisterergasthof.

6 ☐   Follow a side lane past four or five houses, as far as a left-hand bend.

7 ☐   Turn half-right, away from the lane, along a side track leading

to the Bruberstube restaurant.

The Bruberstube could make an early coffee stop in this short valley walk.

8 ☐ Walk down the drive from the Bruberstube and turn right on joining another side road. Follow this past a group of houses as far as the road end.

9 ☐ Bear left at the last house and walk across a meadow, passing beneath a ski-tow cable.

10 ☐ Keep right, then left past the Mayerhofer farmhouse. Follow the lane to a side road. Aim to the right of a house opposite and follow the field path which starts at this point.

11 ☐ Walk towards the bottom station of a ski-tow. Bear left then right by its lower pylon. Cross a small stream and walk along a path which comes out by the Larchenhof restaurant.

The Larchenhof is ideal for lunch. Prices are modest and the food is good. If you are carrying your own picnic and do not wish to eat it in the fields, then the purchase of a drink or maybe soup, usually permits indoor eating in Austrian restaurants and Gasthöfe. Of course, if the place is extra busy you may be politely refused, but normally there is no objection to eating your own food.

12 ☐ Cross the side lane next to the Larchenhof and walk across a series of meadows, descending towards the road.

13 ☐ Turn left down a lane and right at the main road. Walk along it, past the Brucknerhof Hotel.

14 ☐ Left down the lane opposite, following it as far as a cross track. Turn left, slightly uphill towards a group of farm buildings.

15 ☐ Cross the Oberberg road, still uphill and into forest.

16 ☐ Go downhill at point 1152, and skirting the edge of the forest, walk past a ski-jump.

17 ☐ Join the Ramsau Bach and walk along its right-hand bank, keeping to the edge of the pine forest.

There are good views of the Dachstein's south face across the valley from this point.

Near Ramsau, with the Dachstein mountains in the background

18 ☐   Continue along the path, now named the Philosophenweg, as far as the valley road. Turn right along the latter to follow it back to the tourist office.

There is an attractive old watermill below the path about 200yd (183m) short of the road.

The village church stands behind the tourist office and is well worth a visit. On a hot day the open-air swimming pool in the hollow beyond the church, would make an ideal end to the walk.

B • THE KULMBERG AND SATTELBERG HILLS

---

9 miles (14.5km). 4 hours. Moderate.

The low forested ridge which marks the southern limit of the Ramsau basin, offers a pleasant shady walk beneath the spread of ancient pines.

Spectacular views of the Dachstein range are glimpsed tantalisingly from the forest clearings. To the south across the Enns valley and Schladming lie the Hochstein peaks, outliers of the mightier Tauern group of mountains.

Leaving Ramsau and the main road, the walk climbs quickly through the trees to the summit of Kulmberg — 5,207ft (1,282m). Following the wooded crest of the ridge all the way into the Vorberg valley, the route then changes direction to follow a quiet road through open meadowland back to the main road. Across this, the Buchenweg is taken, eastwards, to the far end of the Sattelberg ridge. A fairly short, but steep climb reaches the top of Sattelberg — 4,112ft (1,253m) and its fine views of the eastern Dachstein ridges. At the end of the ridge top path, is the Edelweiss restaurant .

The Route

1 □ Follow the Schladming road out of Ramsau, away from the tourist office and look for a narrow lane marked by a signpost to the Erlbacher restaurant. Turn right from the road and climb this tree-shaded track.

2 □ Keep right at junctions with minor tracks and paths until the Erlbacher restaurant is reached.

Climb a little way, behind the restaurant, to the top of Kulmberg — 4,207ft (1,282m) for a good view of the Dachstein.

3 □ Cross the access road and almost immediately bear left at a footpath junction.

4 □ Start to descend beneath mature pines, along the broad ridge.

5 □ Take the first turning on the left and follow this path, becoming steeper, towards a path junction. Bear left then right, still beneath the

trees until a complex junction of paths is reached, on the edge of the forest.

The views across the Enns valley on a clear day can come almost as a shock to the senses — the scale is so grand. The mountains filling the background are of the Schladminger Tauern group.

6 □   Turn right to follow the edge of the forest, keeping open meadows on your left hand, until the Vorberg road is reached at the Sportalm restaurant, which could be used as either a late coffee or early lunch stop.

7 □   Left along the road, taking a short cut to the left, behind the Fichtenheim Hotel. Continue to follow this quiet side road as far as the main road.

8 □   Turn right at the road for about 100yd (91m). Go left on the Buchenweg, a signposted lane which skirts woodland and meadow as far as the Kielhuberhof Gasthof.

9 □   Turn left, then second right to use minor roads to the east around the spur of the Sattelberg ridge.

10 □   At the lane end, turn left, steeply uphill beneath mature and often stunted pines.

11 □   Turn left on a narrow path, climbing directly to the summit of Sattelberg — 4,112ft (1253m).

Sattelberg is the viewpoint for the east side of the Dachstein.

12 □   Follow the path, walking gradually downhill as far as the Edelweiss restaurant, on the edge of the forest.

13 □   Walk along the road, past the outdoor swimming pool back to the centre of Ramsau.

C • HOCHSTEIN

10 miles (16km). 6 hours. Moderate/Strenuous.

This exciting high-level ridge walk uses the Planei gondola lift from Schladming to reach the Schladminger hut and returns by the Krummholz lift.

Starting at 6,006ft (1,830m) the route follows the ridge, south-east across a series of hills, all over 6,500ft (1,981m), to reach the narrow Hasenkar-Schulter col. Crossing a high combe filled with a tiny lake, a short steep climb reaches the summit of the Hochstein — 8,346ft (2,543m). The final stages of the climb are steep and rocky and can if necessary, be bypassed on an easier path.

Further steep and rocky ground is encountered to the north before a grassy and then tree-covered ridge leads down to the Krummholzhütte. An easy cable ride will then take you down to Haus and a convenient bus back to Schladming.

The Route

1 ☐   The walk starts from the eastern end of Schladming. Take the Schladminger gondola lift from here to its top station.

The old town of Schladming is well worth visiting, so leave plenty of time to inspect its old walls and the remains of the Salzburg Gate, as well as to look at its attractive shops.

2 ☐   Walk ahead to the south-east, along the upper forested slopes, following the gradually narrowing ridge.

3 ☐   The path skirts most of the rocky summit. Follow it all the way to the narrow gap of the Hasenkar-Schulter col.

Sure-footed walkers with a good head for heights should have no problem reaching most of the summits along this ridge. The all-round views are bound to cause delay, so watch the time!

4 ☐   Fork left beyond the col to follow a path across the wide hollow south of the Hochstein. Pass the tiny lake of Kaltenbachsee.

There are no huts along this part of the walk, so perhaps the lake might be used for a refreshment stop. Bathers beware, the water will be icy cold!

5 ☐   Climb to a junction of paths on top of the col at Kaltenbach-Schulter. Turn left, uphill beneath the final slopes of the Hochstein — 8,346ft (2,543m).

A short but very steep scramble leaves the main path on the right, and aims directly towards the summit of Hochstein. If visiting the summit it will be necessary to return to the main route.

6 ☐   Cross the ridge above the Zweishing-Schulter col — 7,814ft (2,381m) and descend slightly to the west of Hochstein.

7 ☐   Climb across the Maralm-Schulten col — 7,184ft (2,189m) then cross a narrow combe to reach the final col, the Kaiblingloch-Schulter — 7,263ft (2,213m).

The section between Kaltenbach-Schulter and beyond the Kaib-lingloch-Schulter is the trickiest part of this walk. The ground is rocky and often steep, so take great care.

8 ☐   Bear right beneath the Kaiblingloch-Schulter and follow the Tauernhohenweg downhill across a scree slope as far as the upper stations of three ski-tows.

9 ☐   Continue downhill, now on grassy slopes as far as the tree line.

10 ☐   Keep left at a path junction, then half right, aiming towards a large TV transmitter mast. Beyond is the Krummholzhütte and the upper station of the cable car to Haus.

11 ☐   Catch the bus from Haus either back to Ramsau, or to Schladming if that is where you have parked your car.

D • THE SCHLADMINGER GLACIER

10 miles (16km). 6–7 hours. Strenuous.
5,021ft (1,530m) descent.

To most of us, the idea of walking on a glacier unguided and unroped, sounds like a course heading towards disaster. Not all glaciers are crevassed-filled horrors, where danger lies in wait for the unwary. Many are simply huge permanent snowfields whose slopes are either non existent or at most gentle. The upper part of the Schladminger is one of these and the route across it will delight everyone who attempts this walk.

Having set the scene of an easy, safe snowfield, it must be pointed out that the Hallstätter glacier immediately to the north and well marked with safety barriers, is crevassed in its lower reaches and, therefore, beyond the realms of simple mountain walking.

Reached by a cable car which climbs almost vertically up the south wall of the Dachstein summits, the Schladminger glacier is used for all-year-round skiing. There is even a summer *langlauf* or cross-country ski-track. Used as a training area by the Austrian Cross Country Ski Team, it is open to anyone wishing to try this exhilarating sport.

Crossing the glacier to the north-east, the marked route of the walk, leaves the snow for an area of wild rocks, their starkness relieved by pockets of brilliantly coloured alpine flowers. Reaching the Guttenberg Haus hut, the route then plunges in an almost unending series of zigzags, down the rocky slope to reach the main valley. This last part of the walk is long and tiring, unfortunately at the end of a long and wonderful day in the high mountains.

The Route

1 □ Take the bus to the road end and then the Dachstein-südwandbahn cable car to its upper station — 8,576ft (2,613m).

A vast snowfield greets you as you step off the cable car; ahead is the Hallstätter glacier and left is the Schladminger and the route.

2 □ Follow the marked way, to the right over the snowfield, keeping to the sides of cross-country and downhill *pistes.*

3 □ Beyond the glacier the ground under foot is rocky and the path indistinct. Follow the white-red-white waymarks.

Alpine flowers fill sunny hollows in this wild rocky place.

4 □ Follow the marked path as far as a path junction on the Feister-Schulter col — 7,214ft (2,198m).

5 □ Walk down the zigzag path to the Guttenberg Haus hut — 7,043ft (2,146m).

The Guttenberg Haus sits in an almost unbelievable position on a tiny alp, high above the valley and beneath the eastern crags of the dolomitic outliers of the Dachstein group. Anyone tempted to stay

The Dachsteinsüdwand and cable car

overnight can easily do so, the beds are comfortable, the food is simple but substantial.

6 ☐   Follow the waymarked path zigzagging steeply downhill across the sunny slopes until the welcome shade of the tree line is reached.

The steep path below the Guttenberg Haus loses something like 3,489ft (1,063m) of height and should be taken gradually, especially if the afternoon is hot. At the bottom of the path, the Faisterer Gasthof comes as a welcome oasis.

7 ☐   On easier gradients walk through meadows, past the Faisterer *Gasthof*, cross the valley road and follow a field path down to the river.

8 ☐   Turn right gently uphill towards the Hotel Post and Ramsau's tourist office.

E • OBERTAL AND THE IGNAZ-MATTISHÜTTE

13 miles (21km). 6–7 hours. Moderate/Strenuous.
2,996ft (913m) ascent.

Post buses conveniently run to some of the remotest parts of the Austrian Alps and this walk takes advantage of the system. On the way out, the long slog up the Obertal valley is avoided by using the bus as far as its terminus at the Tauerngold *Gasthof*. For the return journey another bus calling at the Zeiner *Gasthof* near the end of the Preuneggtal, saves about $6^1/_2$ miles (10.40km) of road walking. Careful planning around bus schedules is, therefore, the key to the successful and less tiring completion of this walk.

The route climbs quickly up the Giglachtal, a side valley away from the Obertal. Soon leaving the forested slopes, it passes beneath the steep arms of the Giglachalm Spitze — 7,719ft (2,352m) and the Kamp Spitze — 7,844ft (2,390m), to reach the Unter and Ober Giglachsee lakes, two exquisite stretches of water in an attractive alpine setting. The Ignaz Mattis hut completes the scene.

Beyond the lakes a short climb reaches the Preuneggsattel col — 6,410ft (1,953m) and from there to the Zeiner *Gasthof*, the way is downhill along an easy track through alpine meadows and shady pine forest.

The Route

1 ☐ Take the post bus from Schladming along the Obertal to the Tauerngold *Gasthof*.

2 ☐ Walk back down the road for a little way and go past a group of farm buildings and over the river.

3 ☐ Climb past two or three more buildings and cross the nearby meadow to reach the pine forest in front.

4 ☐ Follow the woodland path above the Giglach river.

5 ☐ Climb the rocky outcrop then cross the river.

6 ☐ Walk past an old farm at Lackner Alm then re-cross the river. Swing away uphill, still in forest, but over increasingly rocky ground.

7 ☐   Skirt the bottom of a series of crags to reach the prominently sited cross at Knappenkreuz.

8 ☐   On a further tier of crags rejoin the river and also leave the confines of the pine forest.

9 ☐   Walk across the rocky meadows to the old farm at Giglach Alm.

10 ☐   Take the left fork (as facing uphill) in the stream, cross it and walk towards the lower screes on the mountainside opposite.

11 ☐   Fork right (as facing) at the next stream and climb over the boulder field to reach the Unter Giglachsee.

12 ☐   Follow the lake's northern shore as far as the welcome sight of the Ignaz-Mattis hut.

The setting of the hut with its foreground of lake and backcloth of mountains is bound to please photographers. Flower lovers will also appreciate the alpine meadows and rocky places full of their particular blooms.

13 ☐   Follow the path away from the hut and over the col at Preuneggsattel.

14 ☐   Walk down the Preuneggtal along the unsurfaced valley road, passing the Ursprung Alm hut and then scattered hill farms, many of which also serve refreshments.

The walk down the valley is easy, the track crosses quiet meadows bordered by shaded forest and the gradient after the initial descent on either side of the Ursprung Alm hut, is gradual.

15 ☐   Turn right on joining the road, following it as far as the bus stop at the Zeiner *Gasthof.*

The walk can be extended and to avoid road walking follow tracks into the lower valley below Thonner.

F • BENEATH THE DACHSTEIN SUDWAND

$13^1/_2$ miles (22km). 7–8 hours. Strenuous.

This must be the most dramatic walk in the Dachstein region; it follows the foot of the soaring south wall (*Sudwand*) of the limestone massif for most of its length.

Starting at the road end by the lower station of the Dachstein cable car, the walk follows a path skirting the lower screes from below the Hoher Dachstein, the highest point in the range — 9,859ft (3,004m), to the Bishchofsmütze — 8,070ft (2,459m). All the time, the path keeps well above the tree line until it finally plunges down the slopes of Lindeggwald to join the road through Lammertal.

As on the previous walk, careful timing is needed in order to link with the post bus service, both at the start and finish of the walk. The outward journey should create no problems, being simply the regular service to the Dachstein cable car. However, returning by way of Lungötz in Lammertal, then via Radstatt and Schladming to reach Ramsau, needs careful planning. The Lungötz via Radstatt to Schladming journey should be possible even late in the afternoon, but it may then be necessary to take a taxi for the final leg. Of course, if you are fortunate enough to have a volunteer car driver to meet you at the end of the walk, then there will be no problem.

From the bottom station of the cable car the route is well signposted. It follows the Pernerweg path, part of the trans-European long-distance footpath no 4, over a series of cols which link smaller side peaks to the main mass of the Dachstein. Several huts conveniently line the route which is mainly across the open hillside until the Arzbergalm is reached. From here, the way is downhill through forest as far as Lungötz in the Lammertal valley.

The Route

1 ☐   Take the valley bus to the bottom station of the Dachstein cable car.

2 ☐   Climb uphill, away from the station and beneath the cable and aim for the Dachsteinsüdwand hut on the opposite side of the valley.

The steep dolomitic limestone crags of the south wall, tower almost

The Dachsteinsüdwand

vertically overhead.

3 □   Climb a low col above the hut and turn left, then right at a complex of path junctions.

4 □   Walk ahead on the Pernerweg skirting the upper limits of scrubby pine forest.

5 □   Climb a series of zigzags to the col at Tor — 6,672ft (2,033m).

6 □   Descend the rock and scree-covered slopes. Ignore a path crossing and walk beneath the steep wall of the Eiskarlscheid to a path junction.

7 □   Turn right, uphill and over a col in the side ridge.

8 □   Skirt the top of the forest, on an undulating path to the Hof Kugel — 5,566ft (1,696m).

9 □   Follow the contours around the valley head and climb up to the Hofpürgl hut — 5,596ft (1,705m)

The Hofpürgl will make a suitable, probably late, lunch stop.

10 □   Follow the contours to the right then left around the northern slopes of the Marchstein — 5,094ft (1,522m).

11 □   Downhill to the Arzbergalm hut.

12 □   Turn right on the forest road and walk as far as a sharp bend to the right. Do not go all the way round the bend.

13 □   Left, downhill on a valley path and into forest.

14 □   Skirt across the upper slopes and join the valley access road below the clearing of Hagen Alm.

15 □   Follow the road downhill and keep left at a shrine.

16 □   Follow the increasing size of the stream, the Neubach, as far as Lungötz.

17 □   Unless private transport can be arranged, take the bus to Moos in the Enns vallley, then by way of Schladming to Ramsau.

G • ROSSBRAND

$6\frac{1}{2}$ miles (10.5km). 4 hours. Moderate.
2,510ft (765m) ascent.

Here is a walk for a hot day, when the open sun-traps at higher levels might make such walks a hazardous undertaking, especially for anyone whose skin is not accustomed to intense sunshine. Filzmoos, where the route starts and finishes, is in the upper Mandling valley. It is still part of the general Ramsau basin and like Ramsau, nestles beneath the south wall of the Dachstein, protected by the Rossbrand ridge to its south.

The walk is almost entirely in forest before reaching the upper slopes of Rossbrand itself. This is an easy climb, there is a hut on the summit and beyond it the path swings back into a forest whose shade is retained all the way back to Filzmoos.

The Route

1 ☐   Either drive or take the bus into Filzmoos.

This is a short walk and Filzmoos is worth spending a half hour or so, exploring its quaint byways. There are a couple of old watermills to the north of the main street and the church has some delightful paintings.

2 ☐   Walk west along the road as far as the chairlift and turn left along a side lane. Climb through meadowland towards the forest.

3 ☐   Follow the unsurfaced forest road winding uphill to a junction and turn right.

4 ☐   Follow the contours around the hillside as far as a fork in the forest road and turn left.

5 ☐   Still following the contours, walk on towards a stream. Cross over and continue as far as the track junction and a path to the left. Take the latter.

6 ☐   Start to climb, still in forest until the open space of Kar Alm is reached.

The contrast between forest and open space is quite marked. Bird life is different, as is the plant life. In the forest, you may find alpine clematis and others which prefer to grow in shady places, but out on the open alp are all the sun-loving flowers such as gentians, globe flowers, alpenrose, etc.

7 ☐   Bear right past the farmhouse at Kar Alm then left away from its access road on a path which climbs steadily towards the Radstädter hut on the summit of Rossbrand — 5,808ft (1,770m).

The Radstädter hut will make an ideal lunch stop. It is an excellent place to view the western arm of the Dachstein, as well as the Tauern range to the south.

8 ☐   Follow the access road to the left, away from the hut as far as the first bend.

9 ☐   Walk ahead into the forest on the signposted and waymarked path.

10 ☐   Take the left fork after about 100yd (91m) and begin to walk downhill.

11 ☐   Ignore side tracks, mostly forest roads and join the outward route about $1\frac{1}{2}$ miles (2.4km) above Filzmoos.

12 ☐   Turn right and walk out of the forest and across the meadows into Filzmoos village.

H • THE PANORAMAWEG

11 miles (17.7km). 5 hours. Easy/Moderate.

As the title suggests, this is a walk with glorious views. At first they are local and are of the meadows and villas of Ramsau. Beyond the Birnberg road the view is of the eastern Tauern and in particular of the Hochstein group (see the Hochstein walk (C)). The route drops down to the unspoilt village of Weissenbach where timber farmhouses and barns are still used by the descendants of their original builders. Next the path climbs fairly steeply, but soon levels out on a hillside forest road to aim towards the Rössing Berg, a conical outlier of the Dachstein group, without actually climbing its steep forested slopes. An easy track leads down to the main road and the comfortable Lodenwalker restaurant. Paths running parallel to the valley road return to Ramsau.

The Route

1 ☐   Follow the road past Ramsau's church to the open-air swimming pool, then on towards the Edelweiss restaurant and turn right.

2 ☐   Follow the lane as far as the Tauernhof Hotel and turn left.

3 ☐   Continue along the lane across the meadow-covered hillside past trim villas and sturdy farmhouses.

4 ☐   Bear left at the road end, on a footpath which climbs uphill to the pine forest.

5 ☐   Drop down to a track crossing at point 1000. Go over the forest road and bear right.

6 ☐   Walk through forest and out across a stretch of meadowland and cross the road at Neuhäus.

The meadows along this walk prior to haymaking will be filled with flowers.

7 ☐   Go round the hillside then downhill, in and out of forest to a mill by the side of a little stream.

8 ☐   Turn right along the Panoramaweg, following it as far as Weissenbach.

Weissenbach has plenty to offer the curious observer and photographer. There are at least three old watermills, but it also has Gasthöfe and restaurants to refresh tired and hungry walkers.

9 ☐   Go uphill away from the main road, past the church and fork right after about $\frac{1}{4}$ mile (0.4km).

10 ☐   Continue uphill across meadowland and into the forest, then turn left along a forest road.

11 ☐   Climb steeply at first, then follow the contours to the left as far as the Burgstaller *Gasthof.*

12 ☐   Cross the stream, the Knall Bach, then go uphill on the track to the farm settlement at Gerharter.

13 ☐   Follow the track across the Rössing hillside.

The Rössing Berg — 4,418ft (1,346m), is glimpsed above the trees and to the left of the track.

14 ☐   Turn left, downhill to the road near the Lodenwalker *Gasthof*

15 ☐   Right along the road for 150yd (137m) then right again on a path which runs parallel to the road beneath the farmhouses of Almstube.

16 ☐   Walk through forest, above the road which is rejoined at Percht.

17 ☐   Cross the road, walk down to the Ramsau river and turn left along its southern bank.

18 ☐   Follow the keep-fit course back to the centre of Ramsau village.

MPC

TOUR & EXPLORE WITH MPC VISITOR'S GUIDES

Britain
- Chilterns
- Cornwall
- Cotswolds
- East Anglia
- Devon
- Guernsey
- Hampshire &
  the Isle of Wight
- Historic Places of Wales
- Kent
- Lake District
- Northern Ireland
- The North York Moors,
  York & the Yorkshire
  Coast
- Peak District
- Scottish Borders &
  Edinburgh
- Severn & Avon
- Somerset & Dorset
- South & West Wales
- Sussex
- Welsh Borders
- Yorkshire Dales

Europe
- Austria
- Bavaria
- Black Forest
- Brittany
- Corsica
- Dordogne
- Finland
- Florence & Tuscany
- French Coast
- Iceland
- Italian Lakes
- Holland
- Loire
- Normandy
- Norway
- Rhine, Mosel & Eifel
- South of France
- Sweden
- Turkey
- Tyrol
- Yugoslavia:
  Adriatic Coast

also:
- Walking in the Alps
- Walking in Austria
- Walking in Northern
  France

Simply the Best

Our policy of regularly revising MPC Visitor's Guides means that some titles
may be temporarily unavailable, so send for our up-to-date list of these and our
other books.